↭ PRAISE

I'm getting a copy for every member of my RCIA class.

— WILLIAM H. DUQUETTE —
Author of *Vikings at Dino's*

For a long while, Julie Davis has been, as her blog title suggests, one of the happiest Catholics I know. But from where does that happiness stem? Simple. She's encountered Jesus Christ, and the result of such an encounter is always joy. In this reflective new devotional, she helps us meet Jesus in the same way. The wonderful diversity of quotes, prayers, and reflections, taken from the best parts of the Christian spiritual tradition, make it easy to find Jesus in our busy, scattered lives. If you want to be a happy Catholic, you need to encounter Jesus. And if you want to encounter Jesus, read this book.

— BRANDON VOGT —
Author of *RETURN: How to Draw Your Child Back to the Church*

This book is a joyful pilgrimage to the Father, made with the most amazing companions, from Ambrose of Milan to Marshall McLuhan. As always, Julie Davis leads us forward in prayer by way of good books, good movies, good conversation, and even good food. Highly recommended.

— MIKE AQUILINA —
Author of *The Fathers of the Church*

In our fast-paced world, we love the pithy phrase, but we're forever sharing or re-tweeting a striking quote and then moving on, without really pondering why the phrase speaks to us, or what it can bring us. In this book Julie Davis takes those phrases and makes them useful in the most productive way possible — to help us become closer to Christ Jesus. Her brief meditations are down-to-earth, thoughtful, easily Identified with, and truly useful for helping us become open, just a little bit more each day, to the Christ who loves us and wants us to draw nearer to him, that he may drawn nearer to us.

— ELIZABETH SCALIA —
Editor-at-Large at Aleteia.org and author of
Little Sins Mean a Lot: Kicking our Bad Habits Before they Kick Us

From the very first page, where I was gently told to "listen", my prayer life was improved. Is there anything more desirable? What a gift.

— SCOTT DANIELSON —
A Good Story is Hard to Find podcast host

Seeking Jesus in Everyday Life was both a pleasure to read and extraordinarily helpful. Julie Davis has the difficulties of the human heart summed up right there. Beautifully done.

— JENNIFER FITZ —
Author of *Classroom Management for Catechists*

The search for God begins with prayer. In this endearing, practical book, Julie Davis takes us by the hand and leads us to some of the most thought-provoking and heart-inspiring meditations on Jesus ever written. If you're seeking God or feel lost on your spiritual journey, this book is a compass pointing you in the right direction.

— GARY JANSEN —
Author of *Station to Station*

Prayer has never been more accessible or down-to-earth. Let this guide inspire you to talk to God more and better and in the midst of your everyday realness. Julie Davis has put together a gem that is more of an experience than a book.

— SARAH REINHARD —
Author and blogger at SnoringScholar.com

This lovely book by Julie Davis is a collection of quotes, reflections, and prayers designed to deepen our friendship and intimacy with Jesus. When our desire encounters God's grace, our relationship with Jesus grows. Each page is like a springboard for experiencing a greater closeness with our Savior and Lord.

— STEPHEN J. BINZ —
Author of *Threshold Bible Study*

Whether you're a personal prayer novice or simply looking for fresh new resources to draw you into an ever deepening relationship with God, let Julie Davis be your companion as you invigorate your daily dialogue with the divine.

— LISA M. HENDEY —
Founder of CatholicMom.com and author *The Grace of Yes*

SEEKING JESUS IN EVERYDAY LIFE

SEEKING JESUS IN EVERYDAY LIFE

Prayers and Reflections for Getting Closer

BY JULIE DAVIS

author of *Happy Catholic: Glimpses of God in Everyday Life*

NIGGLE
PUBLISHING

**NIGGLE
PUBLISHING**

Copyright © 2017 by Julie Davis. All rights reserved.

Printed in the United States of America
First Printing, 2017

ISBN 978-0-692-86667-2

Niggle Publishing
nigglepublishing.com • julie@glyphnet.com

Cover and page design by Julie Davis
Cover photo - iStock

For Tom, always

⤳ Special Thanks ⤴

I'm grateful to:

Rose Davis

Will Duquette

Erin Schmidt

Patsy Edinburgh

They proofed, encouraged, critiqued — and read the whole darned thing.

∿ CONTENTS ∿

Introduction iii

How to Use This Book vii

∿

Beginning to Pray 1

Looking at Jesus' Many "Faces" 13

Finding Jesus in the Our Father 43

Daily Life with Jesus 61

Getting to Heaven 83

Finding Jesus in the Cross, the Resurrection,
    and the Eucharist 103

Becoming Holy 125

Ways to Pray 147

Battling Evil 177

Finding Jesus Through the Holy Spirit 189

Jesus in the Holy Trinity 199

Continuing to Seek 207

∿

Additional Quotes 211

⋌ INTRODUCTION ⋋

This book is ... solely an expression of my personal search "for the face of the Lord." (cf. Psalms 27:8).

Joseph Ratzinger, *Jesus of Nazareth:*
From the Baptism in the Jordan to the Transfiguration

Like the deer that yearns for running streams,
so my soul is yearning for you, my God;
my soul is thirsting for God, the living God.

Office of Readings, Morning Prayer
Easter Week II, Monday, Cf. Psalm 42: 2-3

ꝯ

This book is for the beginner and for those beginning again — to bring us closer to Jesus, who is every Christian's greatest desire. Have you lost the thrill of those first spiritual experiences? Are you unsure how to connect with Jesus on an everyday basis?

Maybe fellow Christians tell you that Jesus is their best friend, brother, helper in time of trouble, a joyful presence in glad times, and much more. And you're wondering what's wrong with you because you never felt that way.

Or possibly you had that solid connection once and now it's gone. Your "familiar" friend Jesus is nowhere to be found.

You're not alone.

In my own case, I just didn't feel that close to Jesus.

Naturally, I've had some close moments. You can't be a Christian and not have times of connection, sometimes even tinged with a touch of transcendence. But the everyday Jesus, the one who walks beside you? I just didn't feel it.

My head told me he came to be the bridge between us and God, to restore our proper relationship with the divine, and that when we see him we see the Father (John 14:9).

What my heart told me is that a deeper connection to Jesus is key to being a vibrant Christian whose faith keeps growing. I know faith is not just about following your feelings. That way lies disaster. Our feelings can be fickle. But I also felt that Jesus shouldn't be the last person of the Trinity I always turned to.

Was he drawing me to him by being a bit standoffish? Was he right beside me but I couldn't recognize him? Was I not slowing down and spending enough time to connect? I didn't know.

I did know that if Jesus asked me, "Who do you say I am?" then I'd have spent a lot of time stammering before coming up with an answer. That's not right. That's not right at all.

Deeper friendship became my overall prayer goal. I began keeping a notebook of prayers, scripture, and inspirational quotes that might help me to know and love Jesus better. And it began to work. Slowly, gently, gradually, I began to get closer to Jesus.

It took going back to the basics. As Thomas Merton remarked about rereading old journals, "you find out that your latest discovery is something you already found out five years ago. Still it is true that one penetrates deeper and deeper into the same ideas and experiences."

I think this is why we enjoy reading lists like "25 Basics You Must Never Forget" even when we feel like we're experts already. We are reminded of how much we've learned, how much we've forgotten, and how much we're not applying properly.

When I began turning my notes into a book I wondered if anyone would be interested. Then I saw that Pope Benedict XVI (a.k.a. Joseph Ratzinger) wrote the first Jesus of Nazareth book to help draw him closer to Christ. I realized that thousands of years ago the psalmists longed for closeness with God. And I fell into conversation with a friend who said, "Julie, you don't understand. I just don't feel that close to Jesus! I don't know how!"

I do understand. We aren't the first to feel this way. I hope that this book helps all of us to see the face of the Lord.

⌁

Jesus turned, and saw them following, and said to them, "What do you seek?" And they said to him, "Rabbi" (which means Teacher), "where are you staying?" He said to them, "Come and see."

John 1:38-39 (RSV)

⁓ Using This Book ⁓

This book is arranged to lead from the most basic search for Christ into varied, deeper ways to encounter him. Everything is aimed at leading you to encounter Christ in your own way.

Each page contains scripture or an inspirational quote for reflection, a brief commentary, and a prayer. Spend regular time in a quiet place for 10 or 15 minutes each day, or longer if you like. What matters most are your own reflections as you turn your mind and heart to God.

ↄ

The material on each set of facing pages is designed to work together to give a fuller range for reflection.

Whether your eye is drawn first to the right- or left-hand page, both are meant to complement each other for richer insights. The general theme is indicated by the title going across the pages.

Each page also can stand alone for daily prayer so feel free to skip around if you'd prefer.

ↄ

This is about forming a friendship that will last through eternity. Moving through the book will help foster a daily habit of prayer and a way of reflecting that will continue long after you come to the end of this book. Our relationship with Jesus should continue growing throughout our entire lives.

I pray these pages act as a springboard for your own prayers and a deeper friendship with Jesus Christ.

BEGINNING TO PRAY

༄

For me, prayer is a surge of the heart;
it is a simple look turned toward heaven,
it is a cry of recognition and of love,
embracing both trial and joy.

St. Thérèse of Lisieux, Manuscrits autobiographiques

ᔕ Listening ᔕ

I will stand at my guard post,
   and station myself upon the rampart,
I will keep watch to see what he will say to me...

Habakkuk 2:1

ᔐ

Down in my bones, my deepest need is to know Jesus better.

Drawing closer to God, which is the ultimate point of prayer, means I have to listen as well as speak. Ideally I should listen more than I speak.

So, when my prayer time begins, I always read this bit of Habakkuk first. It reminds me that often my duty is to be receptive, to collect myself and push away distractions, to be still. To listen.

ᔐ

Speak, Lord, your servant is listening.

⁓ MEETING GOD

Come Holy Spirit,
fill the hearts of your faithful
and kindle in them
the fire of your divine love.
Send forth your Spirit
and they shall be created
and you shall renew the face of the earth.

Traditional

Into this most intimate relation – God and I – we do not come by speaking, but only by silence; when we are recollected, our inmost soul is opened and the sacred presence can manifest itself. ... We must be serious about this. A life properly lived includes practice in silence.

Romano Guardini, Learning the Virtues That Lead You to God

⁓

"Come Holy Spirit" is a prayer I say before every mass, before every prayer time, and before I read the Bible. In short, it is the prayer that calms and focuses me so I can open my heart and mind to God.

As I seek Jesus, listening for his voice, I turn to the Holy Spirit to help me on the journey.

⁓

Holy Spirit, fill my heart, teach me to listen, and lead me to a deeper love of Jesus.

BACK AT THE BEGINNING ~

In the middle of the journey of our life
I found myself astray in a dark wood
where the straight road had been lost sight of.
Dante Alighieri, The Divine Comedy*

We shall not cease from exploration, and the end of all our exploring will be to arrive where we started and know the place for the first time.
T. S. Eliot, The Four Quartets

~

As I come to Jesus, I think about the fact that I've had to begin again so many times. Does this mean I'm a failure? Shouldn't I have moved past this point for good?

Beginning again can be delightful. The changing of the seasons. A new baby. (Is that why Jesus came to us that way?)

Beginning again can seem too simple, too familiar, or like a waste of time. But if I'm lost, I've got to retrace my steps to get back to "the straight road" I strayed from.

Beginning again can reveal the unexpected. No season is identical. Every baby is unique. Is this why Jesus said we need to be like little children? (Matt. 18:3) The simplest thing is fresh, new, and exciting to their eyes.

It's all in my attitude. Jesus is waiting. I want to begin again.

~

Where have I gone astray? Show me, dear Lord. Lead me in the way of prayer and draw me closer to you.

* translated by Seamus Heaney

◡ "BUT WHAT ABOUT YOU?

"But what about you?" Jesus asked. "Who do you say I am?"

Mark 8:29 (NIV)

◡

Jesus is not just asking the disciples.

He's also asking us. You. Me. Looking into our eyes.

What do I say?

Do I answer automatically? Am I unsure of what to say?

If anyone ever wanted proof that the Bible is a living document used by God to speak to our hearts, this verse settles it. It is immediate. Personal. It puts me on the spot just the way Jesus did to his disciples so long ago.

It is the question of a friend, of someone who wants to be known for himself. There are unspoken vibrations of the question he will ask Peter after his resurrection, "Do you love me?"

That's the point of knowing anyone fully. "Do you love me?"

I must look deep within my heart. I'll see the times he has given me tender love, understanding, and friendship. I'll also see the times I've taken him for granted, ignored him, and haven't listened. "Do you love me?"

◡

Jesus, help me to know you more clearly, love you more dearly, and follow you more nearly.

Who Do You Say I Am?" ᕇ

Everyone wants the key to finding God. But there is no lock!

Father John Libone

ᕇ

This is why there are so many different ways to pray. There is no magic formula for reaching God. It depends on each of us.

God, who created us, doesn't insist on only one style of prayer from his variable, changeable creatures. I can trust him to meet me where I am, in the way I'll be best able to know him.

What is important is that I lift my heart and mind to God.

I may change prayer methods but I must not change that intention.

God never changes. He's there, waiting for me however I pray.

ᕇ

"Ask and you shall receive." I'm here, Jesus. I know you are too. Help me find you.

⌁ Speak as to Your Dearest Friend

When you say only the things that you believe you should say, rather than being honest, any relationship grows cold, including one with God.

James Martin, *Jesus: A Pilgrimage*

Speak with familiarity and confidence as to your dearest and most loving friend. Speak of your life, your plans, your troubles, your joys, your fears. In return, God will speak to you—not that you will hear audible words in your ears, but words that you will clearly understand in your heart.

St. Alphonsus de Liguori*

⌁

When was the last time I spoke to Jesus this directly and honestly? As if I were speaking to my mother or best friend or husband or child?

It's hard. I tend to pray with a request or a specific issue. I certainly don't chat as if I were having a cup of coffee with Jesus. Yet, when I remember to do so, something changes.

Pouring out my thoughts and worries and hopes I let myself laugh and be heartfelt and even get angry with God. It is those moments which make a truthful, personal relationship.

Sometimes it makes me feel silly. But silly moments can be how we learn to love.

⌁

Jesus, today I'm happy ... grateful ... worried ... excited ... frustrated ...

* translation via *Adventures in Daily Prayer* by Bert Ghezzi

In Return, God Will Speak to You ~

Prayer is a work of God but demands commitment and continuity on our part. Above all continuity and constancy are important.

Pope Benedict XVI, General Audience November 20, 2011

Five years of prayer went by. Like any five-year span, it included both good times and bad. ... I prayed through all of it, and the result of my prayers was always the same.

... A shocking sense of vitality and beauty present in both happiness and in the midst of pain. The only thing I can think to compare this experience to is reading a great novel or watching a great movie. The scene before you might be a happy one or a sad one. You might feel uplifted or you might feel heartbroken or you might feel afraid. But whatever you feel, you're still loving the story. Through prayer, I came to experience both pleasure and sorrow in something like that way. In God, the life of the flesh became the story of the spirit. I loved the story, no matter what.

Andrew Klavan, The Great Good Thing

ے

Let's not fool ourselves. I am distant from Jesus because I haven't made enough of an effort to know him. I've not been constant, committed, continuous in prayer.

Not only must I speak to him as my dearest friend, but I must continue to speak. If one person never speaks to the other there can be no conversation and no friendship. That would be a friendship out of balance, out of focus.

Life is out of focus without Jesus.

ے

Draw me to you, dear Lord. Remind me when I forget to pray.

ᴧ: LET ME KNOW YOU

Let me know you, you who know me. Let me know you as I am known, strength of my soul, enter into it, and prepare it for yourself, so that you may have and hold it, without spot or wrinkle.

St. Augustine*

You, Lord, are the object of my love and desire. I blush for myself, and renounce myself, and choose you — for I can please neither you nor myself unless I am in you.

St. Augustine*

ᴧ

These are the words of my heart's dearest longing.

I must make them my prayer.

ᴧ

Lord Jesus, let me know as I am known. I can do nothing where you do not enter in. Enter into my soul.

* translation via *A Year with the Saints* by Paul Thigpen

You Who Know Me ⁓

The prayer preceding all prayer is, "May it be the real I who speaks. May it be the real Thou that I speak to." Infinitely various are the levels from which we pray. Emotional intensity is in itself no proof of spiritual depth. If we pray in terror we shall pray earnestly; it only proves that terror is an honest emotion. Only God Himself can let the bucket down to the depths in us. And, on the other side, He must constantly work as the iconoclast. Every idea of Him we form, He must in mercy shatter. The most blessed result of prayer would be to rise thinking, "But I never knew before. I never dreamed ..."

C. S. Lewis, *Letters to Malcolm: Chiefly on Prayer*

⁓

This is truth itself.

"May it be the real I who speaks. May it be the real Thou I speak to."

How many times I get in the way of the very prayers I speak. "There is no lock!" Except the ones I install myself.

⁓

Jesus, help me to know you more clearly, love you more dearly, and follow you more nearly.

LOOKING AT
JESUS' MANY "FACES"

꒓

Though the New Testament writings
display a many-layered struggle
to come to grips with the figure of Jesus,
they exhibit a deep harmony despite all their differences.

Joseph Ratzinger, Jesus of Nazareth:
From the Baptism in the Jordan to the Transfiguration

᚛ I Desire Only You, Lord ᚜

Certain attitudes deriving from the mentality of "this present world" can penetrate our lives if we are not vigilant. For example, some ... overly prize production and profit; thus prayer, being unproductive, is useless.

Catechism of the Catholic Church, 2727

[Jesus] spoke to Thomas Aquinas from a crucifix hanging in the St. Nicholas chapel: "You have written well of me, Thomas! What do you desire?" Thomas replied, *"Non nisi te, Domine."* Only you, Lord.

Richard John Neuhaus, *The Second One Thousand Years*

ᚄ

I have to return to the beginning often. It doesn't take long for me to forget to listen, to spend time, that I can't force results in prayer. It is about taking my time. It is about remembering the reason I pray every day. I want to be able to say, "I desire only you, Lord."

ᚄ

Show me, Lord Jesus. Draw me closer.

❧ O Most Merciful Redeemer

Thanks be to you, my Lord Jesus Christ,
For all the benefits you have won for me,
For all the pains and insults you have borne for me.

O most merciful Redeemer, Friend, and Brother,
May I know you more clearly,
Love you more dearly,
And follow you more nearly,
For ever and ever.

St. Richard of Chichester, 1197-1253, prayer recorded at his deathbed

❧

Reflecting on this prayer goes a long way toward answering "Who do you say I am?"

It reminds me that Jesus has done me great good at a great cost to himself.

I dwell on what it means that he is my redeemer, my friend, and my brother.

I have meditated on these matters countless times and they remain evergreen. Just as Jesus is himself: inexhaustible and ever new.

To know him more clearly, love him more dearly, and follow him more nearly has become my daily prayer. Easily remembered, always top of mind, and it says it all.

❧

Pray aloud the prayer above.

May I Love You More Dearly ～

Have among yourselves the same attitude that is also yours in
    Christ Jesus,
Who, though he was in the form of God,
    did not regard equality with God something to be grasped.
Rather, he emptied himself, taking the form of a slave,
    coming in human likeness;
    and found human in appearance, he humbled himself,
    becoming obedient to death, even death on a cross.
Because of this, God greatly exalted him
    and bestowed on him the name that is above every name,
    that at the name of Jesus every knee should bend,
    of those in heaven and on earth and under the earth,
and every tongue confess that Jesus Christ is Lord,
    to the glory of God the Father.

Philippians 2:5-11

ↄ

It was eye opening for me that obedience was key to Christ, both
as a fully human person and as the key to his actions glorifying
God. It never really registered until reading these lines.

Jesus came to undo the damage done by Adam's and Eve's
disobedience through his perfect obedience. What does that tell
me about him?

I think of the complete love and trust he has in God the Father's
plan. I think of the tender love he has for us, to make this ultimate
sacrifice. Only such love could inspire such obedience. Only such
love could give it. What a great God and Savior!

ↄ

*May I become like you, dear Lord Jesus, becoming obedient to
God in all things so my days may be lived for His glory.*

↳ To Pray "Jesus"

The divine name may not be spoken by human lips, but by assuming our humanity The Word of God hands it over to us and we can invoke it: "Jesus," "YHWH saves."* The name "Jesus" contains all: God and man and the whole economy of creation and salvation. To pray "Jesus" is to invoke him and to call him within us. His name is the only one that invokes the presence it signifies.

Catechism of the Catholic Church, 2666

In Jesus Christ there is no separation between the medium and the message: it is the one case where we can say that the medium and the message are fully one and the same.

Marshall McLuhan, *The Medium and the Light*

↵

Jesus "translates" God for us. This is profound. I can say his name and it is God's name. Because Jesus is fully God and fully human, his name contains everything to do with that relationship.

When I say Jesus' name I'm not just talking to air. He is literally there with me. In that moment.

"His name invokes the presence it signifies."

I must reflect on that.

↵

Jesus, be with me.

* *Rom* 10:13; *Acts* 2:21; 3:15-16; *Gal* 2:20.

Invokes His Presence ~

I came that they may have life and have it abundantly. I am the good shepherd.

John 10:10-11 (ESV)

Then they said to him, "What must we do, to be doing the works of God?"

Jesus answered them, "This is the work of God. That you believe in him whom he has sent.

John 6:28-29 (NIV)

~

What does it mean to believe in Jesus? It sounds simple.

Believing in Jesus is more than acknowledging he is fully man, fully God, the Son of God. (It's already complicated.) If I believe in Jesus then I should follow him, just like a sheep following the shepherd, in fact.

To believe in Jesus, then, means that I am then called upon to "act" on the commands he gave: to love one another, to forgive, to see Jesus in others.

In fact, I suddenly can see that the whole Catholic faith grew up in an effort to fully "believe in him whom he has sent."

~

Lord I believe. Show me what it means to believe.

⌁ CALL TO ME

Call to me, and I will answer you; I will tell you great things beyond the reach of your knowledge.

Jeremiah 33:3

⌒

Can it be that simple? This is a big promise.

True, it is made to Jeremiah, but in that mysterious way of Scripture, it is also made to you and me.

Will simply asking draw me closer to Jesus? Or to ask it another way, do I dare to believe in Jesus and the promises of God?

⌒

Lord Jesus, answer my search with yourself.

AND I WILL ANSWER YOU ⁓

Jesus came to a town of Samaria called Sychar, near the plot of land that Jacob had given to his son Joseph. Jacob's well was there. Jesus, tired from his journey, sat down there at the well. It was about noon.

A woman of Samaria came to draw water. Jesus said to her, "Give me a drink." His disciples had gone into the town to buy food. The Samaritan woman said to him, "How can you, a Jew, ask me, a Samaritan woman, for a drink?" (For Jews use nothing in common with Samaritans.)

Jesus answered and said to her, "If you knew the gift of God and who is saying to you, 'Give me a drink,' you would have asked him and he would have given you living water."

John 4:5-10

⁓

Jesus is waiting for the Samaritan woman in the middle of her daily routine. The last thing on her mind is an encounter with the living God in the flesh! More than that, Jesus tells her if she'd only have asked, he'd have given her an outrageous gift — the living water.

This is an enactment of the promise made to Jeremiah on the opposite page. How much more direct can Jesus get? He waits for me in the same way, in the middle of my everyday routine. I simply have to see him, to listen, to have that conversation.

⁓

Jesus, I don't know what to ask for except to grow closer to you. Fill me, dear Lord, with the living water and show me the way I should go.

ᵕ Wʜᴀᴛ ɪs Cᴇʀᴛᴀɪɴ ɪɴ Lɪғᴇ ᴀɴᴅ Dᴇᴀᴛʜ?

Yet for us there is
  one God, the Father,
        from whom all things are and for whom we exist,
  and one Lord, Jesus Christ,
        through whom all things are and through whom
        we exist.

I Corinthians 8:6

ᶜ

So few lines. So much meaning.

I think of Genesis with the wind sweeping over the water, the Spirit of God. This is creation of the world, of all things, from the lowest speck of dirt to me myself.

I turn over the many meanings of "from whom … for whom … through whom … we exist."

These words and what they say about God and me are ever true and yet ever changing. Just like God himself. He is a mystery which I seem about to grasp one minute and which eludes me the next. I may never find the end of it but it is work that refreshes.

ᶜ

I will never fully understand you, Lord Jesus. Bring me closer to you as I meditate on my existence in relationship to you.

THE LOVE OF CHRIST ~

If anyone should ask: What is certain in life and death — so certain that everything else may be anchored in it? ... Not people ... or any product of human genius. Also not nature, which is so full of profound deception ... The answer is: The love of Christ. ... Certain is only that which manifested itself on the cross. The heart of Jesus Christ is the beginning and end of all things.

Romano Guardini, *The Lord*

~

The love of Christ is shown to me through the life of Christ.

I am certain that the love of Christ is my anchor to true reality in this world. When I look at life without focusing on Jesus is when I go astray, lie to myself, get fooled.

I am certain that Jesus will be the anchor I cling to at the moment I die. Each of us dies alone. Only Christ bridges that barrier between this life and the next.

It always comes back to the cross. That shadow looms over all. I cannot look away. Not from horror, but in gratitude. The full manifestation of his love is truly on the cross.

~

Help me to see your heart in the cross. Help me to anchor myself in it.

⌁ Think of Prayer

Pray without ceasing.

I Thessalonians 5:17

Think of prayer less as an activity for God and more as an awareness of God. Seek to live in uninterrupted awareness.

Max Lucado, One God, One Plan, One Life

ↄ

When I remember to concentrate on "awareness" instead of
thinking of prayer as an "appointment with God" it's like being in
the room with someone else who's reading a book. You don't have
to talk. You are both aware of each other without words. It makes
everyday life deeper and richer.

That's a whole different sort of prayer. One that I can pray without ceasing.

ↄ

It's good, Lord, to be here with you.

AS AN AWARENESS OF GOD ~

All for the glory of God.

> Come Holy Spirit.

Jesus, be with me.

> Lord, you know all things.
> You know that I love you.

Lord, I believe; help my unbelief

> Speak Lord, your servant is listening.

As for me, I am poor and needy;
but the Lord takes thought for me.

> It's good, Lord, to be here.

~

The traditional way to "pray without ceasing" is to repeat a simple phrase whenever you think of it.

The ones above are the sort that pop into my mind when I want to pray but can't keep my mind on it. It works wherever I am, helping me to feel God near me.

One of my favorites comes to mind often during Mass. That's not a bad time to have, "It's good, Lord, to be here" as the only thing you can think.

~

Jesus, be with me.

◦ THE HEAVENS ARE TELLING

The heavens are telling the glory of God;
    and the firmament proclaims his handiwork.
Day to day pours forth speech,
    and night to night declares knowledge.
There is no speech, nor are there words;
    their voice is not heard;
Yet their voice goes out through all the earth,
    and their words to the end of the world.

Psalm 19: 2-5 (RSV)

Earth's crammed with heaven
and every common bush, afire with God.

Elizabeth Barrett Browning, Aurora Leigh

ᕽ

This is a world full of life. Every single one of us, from the lowest amoeba to a blade of grass to the newest baby, are individual and distinct "selves." Each one has it's own needs and desires.

Every bit is a reflection of God's endless creativity and innate love. All spoken without a single word. I can't get enough of it.

ᕽ

Thank you for the endless beauty and variation that refresh my Spirit and praise your glory, Lord.

THE GLORY OF GOD ~

Mountains and hills shall break out in song before you,
    all the trees of the fields shall clap their hands.

Isaiah 55:15

Beauty descends from God into nature: but there it would per-
ish and does except when a Man appreciates it with worship
and thus as it were *sends it back to God:* so that through his con-
sciousness what descended ascends again and the perfect circle
is made.

C. S. Lewis, letter to Arthur Greaves, 1930

~

I really love those animated descriptions of nature jumping,
clapping, and singing. It's joyful, whimsical, and a wonderful way
to express how their very existence worships the God who made
them. It also connects me with those ancient writers.

My love of nature not only delights me, but defines beauty in a
new way. My appreciation both worships God and makes me a
participant with the cosmos.

That is a new idea for me. It says so much about God's
generosity and the delight, his delight, that comes from sharing in
spontaneous love.

~

*Every bird in a bush, every ant with a heavy load, the wind on
my skin, and the clouds in the brilliant sky all cry out praise to
you. May my life do likewise.*

⌁ When You Seek Me

Indeed, before you [Lord] the whole universe is like a grain
from a balance,
or a drop of morning dew come down upon the earth.
But you have mercy on all, because you can do all things;
and you overlook sins for the sake of repentance.
For you love all things that are
and loathe nothing that you have made;
for you would not fashion what you hate.
How could a thing remain, unless you willed it;
or be preserved, had it not been called forth by you?
But you spare all things, because they are yours,
O Ruler and Lover of souls,
for your imperishable spirit is in all things!
Therefore you rebuke offenders little by little,
warn them, and remind them of the sins they
are committing,
that they may abandon their wickedness and believe in
you, Lord!

Wisdom 11:22-12:2

⌁

The universe is a drop of dew to God. Yet Jesus tells me God
also knows when a sparrow falls and how many hairs are on my
head (Matt. 10:29-30). That's mind blowing. It shows me how vastly
outside my comprehension he is.

I am little in the scheme of things, yet so loved—for my "self"—that
God will warn me little by little so I may turn toward him. How can I
feel anything but loving gratitude for him?

⌁

*Thank you for being the lover of my soul and gently turning me
away from my sins.*

I WILL CHANGE YOUR LOT ~

Where were you when I founded the earth? ...
While the morning stars sang together
and all the sons of God shouted for joy?

Job 38: 4, 7

For I know well the plans I have in mind for you, says the Lord,
plans for your welfare and not for woe! Plans to give you a future
full of hope. When you call me, and come and pray to me, I will
listen to you. When you look for me, you will find me. Yes, when
you seek me with all your heart, you will find me with you, says
the Lord, and I will change your lot.

Jeremiah 29:11-14 (NAB)

ع

This is astonishing. The creator of all creation's got a specific
plan—for me. All he is waiting for is for me to open my heart and
listen. What a gentleman.

This is the honest truth. This is the loving God that Jesus came to
show us in person.

He already has changed my lot. And my heart. And my life. If I
come yearning to know him better, will he not answer?

ع

My heart is full. All I can do is love and worship and praise you.

⤳ THE REASON FOR YOUR HOPE

Always be ready to give an explanation to anyone who asks you
for a reason for your hope.

I Peter 3:15

⤳

Someone steps on the elevator, sees the cross around your neck,
and says, "You're a Christian? Why?"

You've got one minute to give your "elevator faith pitch."

The first time this scenario popped into my head, I panicked. I'd
simply never thought of summing up my faith that way.

How could I not have a quick answer to why I'm a Christian? (I'm
someone who whiles away dull moments thinking "what if" the
zombie apocalypse happened. I love "what if." But this one's
harder. It could actually happen.)

After several days of pondering, I realized what was a blessing
it was to cast my mind over what the Lord has done for me. It
showed me I really do love Jesus more than I realize.

For me, it came down to three reasons. Yours may be different. Be
sure you know the reason for your hope. Considering the question
can give great joy.

⤳

Holy Spirit, I depend on you to teach me what I should say.
see Luke 12:11-12

REASON 1 ~

I have looked for happiness everywhere: in the elegant life of the salons, in the deafening noise of balls and parties, in accumulating money, in the excitement of gambling, in artistic glory, in friendship with famous people, in the pleasure of the senses. Now I have found happiness, I have an overflowing heart and I want to share it with you. ... You say, "But I don't believe in Jesus Christ." I say to you, "Neither did I and that is why I was unhappy.

Hermann Cohen, letter to a friend

~

I'm happy.

All my life I searched for Truth, wondering if there were such a thing. And I found it in Jesus.

~

Think over your history with God and consider the "reason for your hope.

⌁ REASON 2

The man who sins does not do what he likes; he does what sin likes. A man can let a habit get such a grip of him that he cannot break it. He can allow a pleasure to master him so completely that he cannot do without it ... He can get into such a state that in the end, as Seneca said, he hates and loves his sins at one and the same time. So far from doing what he likes, the sinner has lost the power to do what he likes ... this is precisely Jesus' point (John 8:33-36). No man who sins can ever be free.

William Barclay, *Gospel of John Daily Study Bible, vol. 2*

⌁

I'm free.

I still sin but I thank God for the sacrament of confession and renewed strength to begin again when I fail. There is a joy in that. It draws me closer to him.

⌁

Think over your history with God and consider the "reason for your hope.

REASON 3 ~

The good Providence of God cares for me as no one else who exists in the world.

Cardinal Tarcisio Bertone, The Daily Decalogue of Pope John XXIII

~

God loves me.

He doesn't just care about "people." God cares about *me*. He knows me inside and out and loves me despite my flaws and unworthiness.

~

Think over your history with God and consider the "reason for your hope.

⌁ In the Beginning was the Word

In the beginning was the Word, and the Word was with God, and the Word was God. He was in the beginning with God; all things were made through him, and without him was not anything made that was made. ...

And the Word became flesh and dwelt among us, full of grace and truth; we have beheld his glory, glory as of the only Son from the Father.

John 1:1-3, 14 (RSV)

"God, who creates and conserves all things by his Word, provides men with constant evidence of himself in created realities. And furthermore, wishing to open up the way to heavenly salvation — he manifested himself to our first parents from the very beginning."* He invited them to intimate communion with himself and clothed them with resplendent grace and justice.

Catechism of the Catholic Church, 54

⌁

It never ever occurred to me to make the connection between the Word being in the beginning, God the Father's face-to-face friendship with Adam and Eve, and Jesus' becoming man to show us the Truth in person.

What a tag team! It is continual as each of us is created and comes to know Jesus. It reminds me that communion and community have been the plan from the beginning.

⌁

Let me know you, you who know me.

* *DV* 3; cf. *Jn* 1:3; *Rom* 1:19-20.

AND THE WORD BECAME FLESH ~

The Lord created me at the beginning of his work, the first of his acts of old. Ages ago I was set up, at the first, before the beginning of the earth. When there were no depths I was brought forth, when there were no springs abounding with water. Before the mountains had been shaped, before the hills, I was brought forth; before he had made the earth with its fields, or the first of the dust of the world. ... then I was beside him, like a master workman; and I was daily his delight, rejoicing before him always, rejoicing in his inhabited world and delighting in the sons of men.

Proverbs 8: 22-26, 30-31 (RSV)

~

This passage is written about Wisdom, but the Gospel of John and the Fathers of the Church have long portrayed Jesus in the language of Wisdom as found in Proverbs: he existed with God before creation, he rejoices in human beings and desires to be with us, he gives us life.

I wonder if this was one of the passages that Jesus interpreted on the road to Emmaus: "Then beginning with Moses and all the prophets, he interpreted to them what referred to him in all the scriptures." (Luke 24: 27)

Does thinking of Jesus as the master workman, rejoicing in the world and delighting in us, change the way I see Jesus?

~

My heart burns within me when I recognize you in Scripture, Jesus.

❧ Jesus: the Firstborn of All Creation

As white light contains all colors, the Word virtually contains everything distributed over the breadth of the universe, the length of time, the depths of intelligence, the peaks of the ideal. ...

Bearing all this within him, that same Christ entered into history, loved and died in the narrow confines of a human life.
Romano Guardini, The Lord

ↄ

I love this because it helps me to grasp the immensity of what it really means that Jesus is fully God. It helps bring home just how radical the Incarnation really was.

ↄ

Let me know you, you who know me.

AND AS HUMAN AS IT GETS ~

Jesus is as human as it gets: he got exhausted, took naps (although he had nowhere to lay his head), took baths, trimmed his beard, learned to walk and talk, and, as little babies are wont to do, squealed and squirmed with joy during mother-son playtime. ...

We can laugh with the giggling, writhing Christ-child because we know that this be-tickled body is the same body that he will offer freely out of love to go hungry, to walk all up and down Israel, to preach the good news, to heal the sick and the blind, to suffer injustice, to be scourged, to be crucified, to die. ... And in the resurrection, this same body, this same humanity, has risen from the dead and has become all humanity's path to heaven.

> Brother Gabriel Torretta, O.P. , "Did the Virgin Mary
> Tickle the Baby Jesus?," *Dominicana Journal*

~

I love to reflect on this because it helps me connect with Christ as a real human being. Just like me, he had a favorite food, a favorite game, a favorite story.

Does this "face" of Jesus change how I talk to him?

~

Let me know you, you who know me.

∿ "I AM

In him was life, and the life was the light of men. The light shines in the darkness, and the darkness has not overcome it. ...

The true light that enlightens every man was coming into the world. He was in the world, and the world was made through him, yet the world knew him not.

John 1:4-5, 9-10 (RSV)

Jesus spoke to them, saying, "I am the light of the world; he who follows me will not walk in darkness, but will have the light of life.

John 8:12 (RSV)

∿

Coming from a completely secular background, I know what happens when there isn't enough light. You grope for truth, you can't easily distinguish half-truths, you cling to the shadows thinking they are real.

The light of Christ not only awakened me to a fuller life, it illuminated my path. What's even better is that he continues leading me into the mystery of faith which keeps getting richer all the time.

∿

Lead me in your light, Lord Jesus.

THE LIGHT OF THE WORLD" ~

In the same way that Mary gave birth to Jesus, the Light of the World, and yet remained a virgin, light can pass through glass without altering the glass. When the glass is coloured, the symbolism deepens: the light takes on the same colour as the glass, just as God had "passed through" Mary, and took on her nature, humanity, in the form of Jesus.

Richard Stemp, *The Secret Language of Churches & Cathedrals*

~

I think of this every time I look at a stained glass window.

I also think it is a wonderful analogy for how each of us is to be. Each of us is the stained glass that God passes through to shine into the world.

How easy do I make it for others to see the light in me? Do I see that light in them?

~

Use me, dear Lord, to help bring your light into this world.

❧ As Every Woman Begets a Child

Jesus, knit so wonderfully in the womb of Mary ...
have mercy on us.
Jesus, word made flesh, taking on a human body in the womb
of Mary ... *have mercy on us.*
Jesus, whose Precious Blood first flowed through tiny arteries
and veins in the womb of Mary ... *have mercy on us.*
Jesus, hidden nine months in the womb of Mary ...
have mercy on us.
Jesus, begotten by God, nourished by the substance and blood
of His Most Holy Mother in the womb of Mary ...
have mercy on us.
Jesus, leaping from eternity into time, in the womb of Mary ...
have mercy on us.
Jesus, whose Holy Limbs first budded in the womb of Mary ...
have mercy on us.
Jesus, whose Godhead the world cannot contain, weighing only
a few grams in the womb of Mary ... *have mercy on us.*
Jesus, Divine Immensity, once measuring only tenths of an
inch in the womb of Mary ... *have mercy on us.* ...

Litany to Jesus in the Womb of Mary,
Helpers of God's Precious Infants Prayer Book

❧

This makes the Incarnation take on real depth for me. God
become man, Jesus in the womb of Mary, a tiny baby.

It really happened.

❧

Pray the litany aloud.

So Every Child Begets a Mother ∿

As every woman begets a child, so every child begets a mother. The helplessness of the infant, in language stronger than words, solicits the mother, saying: "Be sweet, be self-sacrificing, be merciful." A thousand temptations of a mother are crushed in that one radiating thought: "What of my child?"... The child makes the fatigue and weariness of the mother, as he makes her joy in his success and her agonies in his falls from grace. The child brings the impact of another life, and no mother escapes his vital rays.

Fulton Sheen, *The World's First Love*

ↄ

Because I know the end of the story, I've always thought of Jesus and Mary in picture book form, each with their separate paths.

What is truer, of course, is that each helped form the other. Caring for Jesus changed Mary. Being raised by Mary and Joseph set Jesus on his path as perfect human.

This also makes the Incarnation more real for me. I also think of what a radical plan it was — God becoming man. Becoming baby. Becoming little boy. Becoming teenager.

ↄ

Hail Mary, full of Grace, the Lord is with thee. Blessed art thou among woman and blessed is the fruit of thy womb Jesus.

FINDING JESUS
IN THE OUR FATHER

ﻉ

The words of the Our Father ...
aim to configure us to the image of the Son.

Joseph Ratzinger, Jesus of Nazareth:
From the Baptism in the Jordan to the Transfiguration

ᴠ᙭ GOD WAS ALWAYS LIKE JESUS ᙭

In the beginning was the Word, and the Word was with God,
and the Word was God. He was in the beginning with God.

Gospel of John 1:1-2 (RSV)

If the word was with God before time began, if God's word is
part of the eternal scheme of things, it means that *God was always like Jesus.*

William Barclay, *Gospel of John Daily Study Bible, vol. 1*

ᒃ

First, this astonishes me. It's one of those things that I always
should have known, but that didn't occur to me, God was always
like Jesus.

What is it that I think I "know" about God which I can then use to
know Jesus better? Or vice versa?

ᒃ

Show me, Lord Jesus. Help me to see you more closely.

◡ The Perfect Prayer

I am the man who with utmost daring discovered what has been
discovered before.

G. K. Chesterton, Orthodoxy

Our Father, Who art in heaven,
Hallowed be Thy Name.
Thy Kingdom come.
Thy Will be done, on earth as it is in Heaven.
Give us this day our daily bread.
And forgive us our trespasses,
as we forgive those who trespass against us.
And lead us not into temptation,
but deliver us from evil. Amen.

◡

After I became Christian, one of the first things that attracted me
was the Our Father prayer.

I pondered it as a whole. I pondered each line alone. Every which
way I looked it couldn't be bettered. I concluded that this was the
perfect prayer. I was pretty proud of myself for figuring this out.

It wasn't long before I realized that perfection was "discovered"
soon after the Church began. (D'oh!) After all, God himself gave it
to us and people immediately understood that made it special.

That humbled me. And made me laugh at myself. Not a bad
beginning as a Christian!

◡

*Thank you Jesus for giving us the perfect prayer. Teach me to pray
with my whole being.*

THE "OUR FATHER" ～

Run through all the words of the holy prayers [in Scripture], and I do not think that you will find anything in them that is not contained and included in the Lord's Prayer.

St. Augustine, Letter 130

～

The Our Father seems the ideal prayer for my personal meditation. If Jesus thought these were "the basics," then it also tells me something about him. When I pray it, I need to slow down, and not rattle it off thoughtlessly.

We'll consider the Our Father petition by petition. You'll see quite a few thoughts from the Catechism and Jesus of Nazareth, which I find particularly thought provoking for meditations which draw us closer to Christ through the prayer he taught us.

～

May knowledge of you, dear Father, in me be made bright so that I may love you with my whole heart, desire you with my whole soul, and direct all my intentions to you.

Adapted from St. Francis of Assisi's Meditation on the Our Father

☙ OUR FATHER

Prayer is not a kind of magic, but entrusting ourselves to the Father's embrace.

Pope Francis, *Encountering Truth*

He who sees me sees the Father.

John 14:9 (RSV)

ↄ

Some have had good fathers. Others have not.

All of us, though, carry an ideal vision of what a good father would be like. That vision comes from our Father in Heaven. It is infused in our hearts so we can always recognize him. Jesus came to show us the father in person.

He is my father. He is yours. He is *ours* and that makes us family. We can talk to him about anything and everything because he loves and understands us wholly.

ↄ

May knowledge of you, Father, in me be made bright.

Who Art in Heaven ~

Father, they are your gift to me. I wish that where I am they also may be with me, that they may see my glory that you gave me, because you loved me before the foundation of the world.

John 17:24

This mystery of blessed communion with God and all who are in Christ is beyond all understanding and description. Scripture speaks of it in images: life, light, peace, wedding feast, wine of the kingdom, the Father's house, the heavenly Jerusalem, paradise: "no eye has seen, nor ear heard, nor the heart of man conceived, what God has prepared for those who love him."*

Catechism of the Catholic Church, 1027

~

What does it say about God's fatherhood that he is in heaven?

What does it say about Jesus as Son of God, Son of Man, that he is in heaven?

What does it say about me, that heaven is my true home since my father is there?

~

May knowledge of you, Father, in me be made bright.

* *1 Cor* 2:9.

ᵛ HALLOWED BE THY NAME

The term "to hallow" is to be understood here ... to recognize as holy, to treat in a holy way. And so, in adoration, this invocation is sometimes understood as praise and thanksgiving.*

Catechism of the Catholic Church, 2807

How do I treat God's holy name? ... Do I take care that God's holy companionship with us will draw us up into his purity and sanctity, instead of dragging him down into the filth?

Joseph Ratzinger, Jesus of Nazareth:
From the Baptism in the Jordan to the Transfiguration

ᶜ

Jesus gave us this phrase. I think of Jesus' total trust and obedience, of his closeness to the Father. It is humbling to think of the difference between Jesus' love of God and the way I sometimes treat both of them fairly casually.

"How do I treat God's holy name?"

ᶜ

May knowledge of you, Father, in me be made bright.

* Cf. *Ps* 111:9; *Lk* 1:49.

Thy Kingdom Come ᷉

Thy Kingdom Come:
so that Thou may reign in us by grace
and make us come unto Thy Kingdom,
where vision of Thee is made manifest,
love of Thee made perfect, company with Thee blessed,
enjoyment of Thee everlasting.

St. Francis of Assisi, Meditation on the "Our Father"

᷉

If God has a kingdom, then our father is the king. What does it mean to be a child of the king, a prince or princess? Does it change how I see myself and my work for the kingdom?

The upcoming phrase "on earth as it is in heaven" makes it important that my life helps bring God's kingdom here and now.

᷉

Direct all my intentions to you, Father.

ᴠᴥ Thy Will Be Done

In the realm to which we direct our prayer reigns not only su-
preme justice, power, and order, but also the love of the living
God. This love He bestowed on us in absolute freedom. In our
prayers we take our needs and wishes to God, beseeching Him
to act in accordance with the sovereign decisions of His love.
The sentence, "Not as I will, but as Thou wilt," ultimately means
"may Thy love prevail."

Romano Guardini, *The Art of Praying*

ᒑ

I trust that God knows better than I do. I never thought about "Thy
will be done" in terms of what motivates God's will.

That motivation is love as Jesus shows us with his words, actions,
and prayers.

ᒑ

Help me to remember that your will comes from pure love.

On Earth as It is in Heaven ~

Two things are immediately clear from the words of this petition: God has a will with and for us and it must become the measure of our willing and being; and the essence of "heaven" is that it is where God's will is unswervingly done. Or to put it in somewhat different terms, where God's will is done is heaven.

Joseph Ratzinger, *Jesus of Nazareth:*
From the Baptism in the Jordan to the Transfiguration

~

If I live as my truest self and God's will is being done through me, then do I bring a bit of heaven to earth?

God came into time, became one of us, for that very reason: "Thy will be done on earth as it is in heaven."

~

Set me aflame with desire to do your will.

❧ Give Us This Day

While [the Lord] says to his disciples, "Do not be anxious about your life, what you shall eat" (Matthew 6:25), he nevertheless invites us to pray for our food and thus to turn our care over to God.

Joseph Ratzinger, *Jesus of Nazareth:*
From the Baptism in the Jordan to the Transfiguration

ↄ

Sometimes I think of this line as being about the Eucharist. That's how a lot of the Church Fathers have seen it.

Usually, though, I think of it as daily necessities. That's how the regular folk who Jesus taught would have seen it. Honestly, in hard times that's how I see it. I have to be able to know that when trying my hardest isn't working, God will provide.

It's about trust.

ↄ

May I trust you with my whole heart, Lord.

Our Daily Bread ᘔ

And he said to them, "I have eagerly desired to eat this Passover with you before I suffer.

Luke 22:15

If it is "daily bread," why do you take it once a year? ... Take daily what is to profit you daily. Live in such a way that you may deserve to receive it daily. He who does not deserve to receive it daily, does not deserve to receive it once a year.

St. Ambrose of Milan

ᘔ

Jesus longed for the moment when he could come to us in the intimacy of a meal, of bread and wine. He wants to nourish us in the most basic way possible.

How do I approach Jesus in the "veil" of the Eucharist? Do I treat it as automatic? Do I long for Jesus?

ᘔ

May I long for you, as you long for me.

⌁ Forgive Us Our Trespasses As We

Forgiveness exacts a price—first of all from the person who forgives. He must overcome within himself the evil done to him; he must, as it were, burn it interiorly and in so doing renew himself.

Joseph Ratzinger, *Jesus of Nazareth:*
From the Baptism in the Jordan to the Transfiguration

Thus the Lord's words on forgiveness, the love that loves to the end,* become a living reality.

Catechism of the Catholic Church, 2843

⌁

I never thought about the idea that when I forgive someone I am bringing to life Jesus' words about loving to the end. It's humbling and also an honor to be part of that living legacy.

What I do know is that I count on God's limitless understanding and forgiveness. I confess honestly and I take his love for granted. If I have been pardoned, how can I not try my hardest to extend that mercy to others I encounter?

⌁

Thank you for your mercy and loving kindness, dear Father.

* Cf. *Jn* 13:1.

FORGIVE THOSE WHO TRESPASS AGAINST US ∾

And when they came to the place which is called The Skull, there they crucified him, and the criminals, one on the right and one on the left. And Jesus said, "Father, forgive them; for they know not what they do."

Luke 23:33-34 (RSV)

Be not disturbed that you cannot make others as you wish them to be, since you cannot make yourself as you wish to be.

Thomas a Kempis, The Imitation of Christ

ૐ

I take this seriously, I really do. I want to be forgiven and that means I must forgive others.

If only I didn't keep having others' offenses toward me pop into my head in so many different ways. That's when I discover that perhaps my forgiveness isn't as perfect as I thought. I haven't "burned it interiorly."

Then I have to begin again. Because God's forgiven me endlessly too. It was for my sake he was crucified, after all.

ૐ

May I truly love my enemies for your sake, dear Father, and direct all my intentions to you.

⁖ And Lead Us Not Into Temptation

It is difficult to translate the Greek verb used by a single English word: the Greek means both "do not allow us to enter into temptation" and "do not let us yield to temptation."*

Catechism of the Catholic Church, 2846

We are helped a further step along when we recall the words of the Gospel: "Then Jesus was led up by the Spirit into the wilderness to be tempted by the devil" (Matthew 4:1). Temptation comes from the devil, but part of Jesus' messianic task is to withstand the great temptations that have led man away from God and continue to do so.

Joseph Ratzinger, *Jesus of Nazareth:*
From the Baptism in the Jordan to the Transfiguration

"Lead us not into temptation" often means among other things, "Deny me those gratifying invitations, those highly interesting contacts, that participation in the brilliant movements of our age, which I so often, at such risk, desire."

C. S. Lewis, *Reflections on the Psalms*

⁕

I never could understand this. I couldn't reconcile God as "all good" with someone who would "lead me into temptation."

Pope Benedict XVI (Ratzinger) led me to read the Book of Job where temptation is allowed on a massive scale. Those examples have helped mightily with my own trust in God when temptations arise, especially the temptations that I am not equipped to handle.

⁕

My hope is in you, dear Father.

* Cf. *Mt* 26:41.

But Deliver Us From Evil ~

I do not ask that you take them out of the world but that you keep them from the evil one.

Jesus' prayer before his Passion, John 17:15

In this petition, evil is not an abstraction, but refers to a person, Satan, the Evil One, the angel who opposes God. The devil *(diabolos)* is the one who "throws himself across" God's plan and his work of salvation accomplished in Christ.

Catechism of the Catholic Church, 2851

~

I can't remember where I first came across this nugget of information, but I've known almost since I converted that "evil" in this prayer means "the evil one." The devil. The liar. The enemy.

That explains why in my head, the Our Father goes, "Deliver us from The Evil One."

~

Deliver us, Lord, we beseech you, from every evil and grant us peace in our day, so that aided by your mercy we might be ever free from sin and protected from all anxiety, as we await the blessed hope and the coming of our Savior, Jesus Christ.

Roman Missal, *Embolism after the Lord's Prayer*

ᐳ Amen ᐸ

In Hebrew, amen comes from the same root as the word "believe." This root expresses solidity, trustworthiness, faithfulness. And so we can understand why "Amen" may express both God's faithfulness towards us and our trust in him. ...

Jesus Christ himself is the "Amen." He is the definitive "Amen" of the Father's love for us. He takes up and completes our "Amen" to the Father: "For all the promises of God find their Yes in him."

Catechism of the Catholic Church, 1062, 1065

᷎

Every step of the way through the Our Father, I found Jesus awaiting me.

So I shouldn't be surprised that he is here at the end and even is the meaning of the end, "I believe."

Yes, Jesus is the ultimate sign and source of belief in God, the Lord, the Father.

"He takes up and completes our 'Amen'" as he takes up and completes me myself. All I have to do is let him.

᷎

Glory be to the Father, the Son and the Holy Spirit.
As it was in the beginning, is now, and ever shall be, world
without end. Amen.

DAILY LIFE WITH JESUS

O God, from whom all good things come,
grant that we, who call on you in our need,
may at your prompting discern what is right,
and by your guidance do it.

Collect, Tenth Sunday in Ordinary Time

⌁ Living in a Transparent World ⌁

Life is this simple: we are living in a world that is absolutely transparent and the divine is shining through it all the time. This is not just a nice story or a fable, it is true.

Thomas Merton, final address as novice master, 1965

You mean that the whole world — the whole world with the sea, the sky, with the rain, the clouds — the whole world is a metaphor for something else?

Mario, *Il Postino* film

If life is really as simple as Thomas Merton says then why do I lose my way so often?

I get caught up in the details of life, forgetting that Jesus is shining through them if I slow down, open my eyes, take time to let God's small, still voice sound in my ears. I must remember to keep watch on the ramparts.

You are always there, dear Lord. Help me to remember to listen.

⌁ We Want to be Comfortable

To put it simply: the Holy Spirit bothers us. Because he moves us, he makes us walk, he pushes the Church to go forward. ... he is that wind which comes and goes and you don't know where. He is the power of God, he is the one who gives us consolation and strength to move forward. But: to move forward! And this bothers us. It's so much nicer to be comfortable.

Pope Francis, *Encountering Truth*

⌁

I know the excitement and fervor of my encounters with God. And we know what we must do. We promise and mean it. Then comes the daily effort of carrying out those promises. That's when I'd rather be comfortable. I begin making excuses.

That's the difference between me and the saints, I suppose. They listen and move forward no matter what. I must allow myself to be bothered, to move forward.

⌁

Say a prayer to your patron saint asking for their prayers and guidance in moving forward at the Spirit's nudging.

But the Holy Spirit Bothers Us ∾

It was not you who chose me, but I who chose you and appointed you to go and bear fruit that will remain, so that whatever you ask the Father in my name he may give you. This I command you: love one another.

John 15:16-17

∾

This is the movement that the Holy Spirit wants.

To bear fruit.

To trust and turn to the Father in need.

To love one another.

This does not seem like a long or difficult list. How terrible to "want to be comfortable" more than to do these things as I go through daily life.

∾

Lord Jesus, I want to love you and your commands more than my own comfort. Grant me the grace to recognize my selfishness and to go forward anyway.

❧ All Must Be Loved

The turbulent have to be corrected, the faint-hearted cheered up, the weak supported; the Gospel's opponents need to be refuted, its insidious enemies guarded against; the unlearned need to be taught, the indolent stirred up, the argumentative checked; the proud must be put in their place, the desperate set on their feet, those engaged in quarrels reconciled; the needy have to be helped, the oppressed to be liberated, the good to be encouraged, the bad to be tolerated; all must be loved.

St. Augustine, "On the Anniversary of His Ordination"

❧

St. Augustine is describing his daily life here. I bet this looks all too familiar to every parish priest.

The thing is, it's not just priests and religious who should relate to this. It reads like marching orders for every Christian.

The trick is how to do it without wearing out and without becoming a turbulent, argumentative busybody. (I could easily slip up there.)

The answer is: "all must be loved." That's the key to everything.

❧

Dear Lord, help me to live like Augustine.
St. Augustine, pray for us!

I Can Do All Things in Him ～

Brothers and sisters:
I know how to live in humble circumstances;
I know also how to live with abundance.
In every circumstance and in all things
I have learned the secret of being well fed and of going hungry,
of living in abundance and of being in need.
I can do all things in him who strengthens me.

Philippians 4: 12-13 (NAB)

～

This is the description of how to live a Christian life. Period.

The funny thing is that the more hardships I face with Christ at my side, the more I understand how Paul could do this. It isn't a matter of practice making me perfect. It's a matter of being forced to depend on Christ. And of finding that he actually does strengthen me and give me his peace.

It's often by fits and starts but I attribute that to my lack of openness and cooperation, not to Christ. He's there. I just don't always remember to lean on him.

～

Dear Lord, help me to live like Paul.
St. Paul, pray for us!

∴ This Commandment

For this commandment which I command you this day is not too hard for you, neither is it far off. It is not in heaven, that you should say, "Who will go up for us to heaven, and bring it to us, that we may hear it and do it?" Neither is it beyond the sea, that you should say, "Who will go over the sea for us, and bring it to us, that we may hear it and do it?" But the word is very near you; it is in your mouth and in your heart, so that you can do it.

Deuteronomy 30:11-14 (RSV)

The point I want to make is that a woman can achieve the highest spirituality and union with God through her house and children, through doing her work which leaves her no time for thought of self, for consolation, for prayer, for reading, for what she might consider development. She is being led along the path of growth inevitably.

Dorothy Day, *On Pilgrimage*

↵

Even as far back as Deuteronomy we see God reminding everyone that he's not asking more than they can do.

Human nature never changes does it?

That's something for me to remember when I'm dragging my feet obeying. It is not only about actions. It is about my intentions when I act. It is about everyday life, lived to the fullest.

It isn't too hard. I'm just unwilling.

↵

Dear Lord, remind me that you are near and that what you ask is not too hard for me.

— Seeking Jesus in Everyday Life —

Is Not Too Hard for You ~

Do you ask, "What is faith in him?" I answer, the leaving of your own way, your objects, your self, and the taking of His and Him ... *and doing as He tells you.* I can find no words strong enough to serve the weight of this necessity — this obedience.

George MacDonald, *The Truth in Jesus*

We ought not to be weary of doing little things for the love of God, who regards not the greatness of the work, but the love with which it is performed.

Brother Lawrence, *The Practice of the Presence of God*

~

"Doing as he tells you."

Sometimes that is incredibly hard, even when it is a little thing like folding the laundry, dropping my own plans for someone else's, or not grumbling about working overtime. Those things are also God's work when they are done with that intention and with love.

I must do as he tells me. With love.

~

Help me to look outward and obey, Jesus, not to turn inward and only think of what I want.

❧ Only for Today

Only for today, I will seek to live the livelong day positively without wishing to solve the problems of my life all at once.

Only for today, I will take the greatest care of my appearance: I will dress modestly; I will not raise my voice; I will be courteous in my behavior; I will not criticize anyone; I will not claim to improve or to discipline anyone except myself.

Only for today, I will be happy in the certainty that I was created to be happy, not only in the other world but also in this one.

Only for today, I will adapt to circumstances, without requiring all circumstances to be adapted to my own wishes.

Only for today, I will devote ten minutes of my time to some good reading, remembering that just as food is necessary to the life of the body, so good reading is necessary to the life of the soul.

St. John XXIII's Decalogue, part 1

❧

Every morning I pray this entire decalogue aloud. Some days I need the warnings. Some days I need the encouragement. Every day it shows me the footsteps I will try to follow.

❧

Thank you Lord for these sensible prayers that help me follow in your footsteps.

I WILL ... ∿

Only for today, I will do one good deed and not tell anyone about it.

Only for today, I will do at least one thing I do not like doing; and if my feelings are hurt, I will make sure that no one notices.

Only for today, I will make a plan for myself: I may not follow it to the letter, but I will make it. And I will be on guard against two evils: hastiness and indecision.

Only for today, I will firmly believe, despite appearances, that the good providence of God cares for me as no one else who exists in this world.

Only for today, I will have no fears. In particular, I will not be afraid to enjoy what is beautiful and to believe in goodness. Indeed, for twelve hours I can certainly do what might cause me consternation were I to believe I had to do it all my life.

St. John XXIII's Decalogue, part 2

∿

This prayer is one of the best ways I know to live in the present moment. It focuses on what I can do, today, not in some nebulous time in the future. I need to remember that today is where I live and where God meets me.

∿

Thank you Lord for these sensible prayers that help me follow in your footsteps.

~: BEING INCONVENIENCED AND PUT UPON

The apostles gathered together with Jesus and reported all they had done and taught. He said to them, "Come away by yourselves to a deserted place and rest a while." People were coming and going in great numbers, and they had no opportunity even to eat. So they went off in the boat by themselves to a deserted place.

People saw them leaving and many came to know about it. They hastened there on foot from all the towns and arrived at the place before them. When he disembarked and saw the vast crowd, his heart was moved with pity for them, for they were like sheep without a shepherd; and he began to teach them many things.

Mark 6: 30-34

~

I wonder how the apostles felt? They were bursting with their own stories, tired, hungry, and probably had been looking forward to having Jesus to themselves.

Were they used to being put off as Jesus served the crowd? Were they envious or annoyed? How do I react in similar circumstances?

~

Guide my innermost desires, Lord Jesus, so that I may think of others before myself.

For the Good of Others ~

St. Angela of Foligno said that penances voluntarily undertaken are not half so meritorious as those imposed on us by the circumstances of our lives and cheerfully borne. ... Most of us have not the courage to set out on this path wholeheartedly, so God arranges it for us.

Dorothy Day, *On Pilgrimage*

It is one of those rare instances where Jesus's stated intent is thwarted by the needs of the crowd. ... There is no shade of annoyance in Jesus' attitude despite the crowd's thwarting his desire to rest. He begins to teach at once ... when it came to being inconvenienced and put upon for the good of others, he gave us all a sterling example of self-sacrifice.

Roland J. Faley, *Footsteps on the Mountain*

~

I know myself well enough to realize that, unlike Jesus, I'd have been moved with pity for *myself* the second I saw that big crowd appear out of nowhere.

I tend to think about Jesus being in control of his destiny, always in accordance with the Father's plan. This rare glimpse of Jesus with the rug yanked out from under him is the reminder not only of how I need to act, but that Jesus experienced all the same daily problems that I do.

How do I act? How well do I follow his example?

~

Guide my innermost desires, Lord Jesus, so that I may think of others before myself.

❧ THE WORLD WILL ALWAYS BE

Food is the daily sacrament of unnecessary goodness, ordained for a continual remembrance that the world will always be more delicious than it is useful.

Robert Farrar Capon, The Supper of the Lamb

Human beings, at their most human, do things which make no sense to economists. They fall in love. They take vows of poverty, chastity and obedience. They write sonnets, paint cave walls, invent break dancing and perform thought experiments about relativity during their lunch hours working at the patent office. They go Maying, frittering away a perfectly useful day of productive work just to romp in the sun, eat heartily, and thank God for the fact that grass is green, wind is sweet, the universe is a strange place, and life is a gift.

Mark P. Shea, Catholic and Enjoying It blog

❧

I've heard "experts" float the idea of food pills more than once. Killjoys. What would take the joy out of life more than never biting into a peach, melting chocolate on your tongue, or sipping lemonade? I wonder what Jesus' favorite food was?

I especially love that we need to eat several times a day, enjoying tastes, textures, and an infinite variety of dishes invented around the world. In my modern world of efficiency, I need this reminder that God's ideas about living life are larger … and delicious.

❧

Thank you for giving us so much beauty, variety, and deliciousness in our world.

More Delicious Than It is Useful ～

Now there were six stone water jars there for Jewish ceremonial washings, each holding twenty to thirty gallons. Jesus told them, "Fill the jars with water." So they filled them to the brim.

Then he told them, "Draw some out now and take it to the headwaiter." So they took it.

And when the headwaiter tasted the water that had become wine, without knowing where it came from (although the servers who had drawn the water knew), the headwaiter called the bridegroom and said to him, "Everyone serves good wine first, and then when people have drunk freely, an inferior one; but you have kept the good wine until now."

John 2:6-10

～

The miracle at Cana is Jesus' first one so it is hugely significant.

What does it show us about the world God sees and who he is? I see a love of friends, celebration, good wine, and overflowing generosity (almost 200 gallons worth).

I see Jesus showing us that God made a world made to be more delicious than useful. It makes me understand why heaven is so often referred to as a banquet.

～

Thank you, Lord, for the bounty you show us in every way.

⌁ WHAT WILL IT PROFIT A MAN

Then Jesus said to His disciples, "If anyone wishes to come after Me, he must deny himself, and take up his cross and follow Me.

For whoever wishes to save his life will lose it; but whoever loses his life for My sake will find it.

For what will it profit a man if he gains the whole world and forfeits his soul? Or what will a man give in exchange for his soul?

For the Son of Man is going to come in the glory of His Father with His angels, and will then repay every man according to his deeds."

Matthew 16:24-27

⌁

Jesus is saying is that I have to follow him with my whole heart. I'm not allowed to hold back even a little. It's all or nothing.

There are those who give all by literally giving up their lives and becoming martyrs. There are those who give their lives serving others as Mother Teresa did in Calcutta.

Then there are the rest of us. We are disciples too in our ordinary, workaday lives. Jesus is once again looking you and me in the eyes, asking for our answer. Nothing but a whole heart is enough.

⌁

Dear Lord, I want to follow you with a whole heart. Help me to see where I'm blind. Where am I holding back?

TO GAIN THE WORLD AND LOSE HIS SOUL? ∿

The people who have a strong sense of love and belonging believe they're worthy of love and belonging. ... These folks had, very simply, the courage to be imperfect.

They fully embraced vulnerability. They believed that what made them vulnerable made them beautiful. They didn't talk about vulnerability being comfortable, nor did they really talk about it being excruciating ... They just talked about it being necessary. They talked about the willingness to say, "I love you" first, the willingness to do something where there are no guarantees ... to invest in a relationship that may or may not work out. They thought this was fundamental.

Brené Brown, "The Power of Vulnerability," TED Talk

ↄ

As life with Christ has changed me over time, I've learned that what Brené Brown says is absolutely true.

It's risky. It can be terrifying. But that vulnerability, that courage to be imperfect, is absolutely the only way for my life to be happy. It's how I can admit to my kids that I was wrong, how I can risk myself making a new friend, how I can overcome the fear of dance classes.

These are small things that don't seem like "taking up the cross" but they can be paralyzing if we don't allow ourselves to be vulnerable. And they are all ways that we practice carrying smaller crosses so we've got the muscles to carry big crosses that come our way.

ↄ

Lord, I love you. Grant me the strength and courage to live my life fully and truthfully.

⤞ I Have Given You An Example

When you desire to advance in the perfection of some virtue ...
First, adore in Christ the virtue you've chosen. Reflect on how
excellent he was in it, and how perfectly he practiced it throughout his whole life.

St. John Eudes*

For I have given you an example, that you also should do just as
I have done to you.

John: 13:15 (RSV)

৴

I am not sure why St. John Eudes' advice surprised me. Perhaps
it's because my problems tend to be things like snapping at my
husband or watching TV instead of cooking dinner. I think of
Jesus in terms of "big" virtues not in terms of small virtues which I
struggle with.

This made me look more closely at my own actions. Snapping at
my husband means I need to be more patient. Goofing off instead
of doing my chores means I need to put the good of others ahead
of my own selfish desires. Jesus did give me a perfect example of
those virtues.

What seems small to me actually winds up being part of the big
picture. Jesus' life and actions really do translate down to every
part of my own.

৴

*Jesus, help me to remember that there is no action of mine so small
that I cannot see your example shining through to lead me.*

* translation via *A Year with the Saints* by Paul Thigpen

Do Just As I Have Done ~

Each vice deceives with a false and shadowy beauty.

Pride makes a pretense of superiority. But you alone, Lord, are the highest over all.

What does ambition seek except honor and glory? But you alone, Lord are the highest over all. ...

Envy contends for excellence. But what is so excellent as you, Lord? ...

Anger seeks revenge. But who avenges more justly than you, Lord? ...

Thus the soul is unfaithful when it turns away from you, Lord, seeking those things without you, which it can find pure and untainted nowhere until it returns again to you. In this way, all those who separate themselves against you nevertheless perversely imitate you.

St. Augustine, *Confessions*

ح

Sometimes turning something on its head gives us a new way to understand. When I contemplate how my vices distort God's goodness, then I strive to return to the true, untainted path. It gives me renewed energy to embrace the virtues that show me the truth.

ح

Keep my vision clear and my eyes fixed on you, Lord Jesus.

☙ FORGIVE THEM

When they came to the place called the Skull, they crucified him there, along with the criminals—one on his right, the other on his left. Jesus said, "Father, forgive them, for they do not know what they are doing."

Luke 23: 33-34 (NIV)

That particular phrase helped me a great deal with the Jesuit who wouldn't speak to me. He didn't seem to know what he was doing. Indeed, people who sin sometimes don't seem to be thinking clearly.

James Martin, *Seven Last Words*

↶

James Martin's insight was key for me, just when I was struggling with forgiving someone. And that made Jesus' forgiveness during his crucifixion really come alive. The Pharisees and Sadducees thought they were doing the right thing. It takes a bigger view to give us the context in which to see that they weren't thinking clearly.

My view is often not clear. I need Jesus to give me the big picture, the proper perspective. And if I have that problem, obviously so can my enemies. Keeping that idea of "not thinking clearly" has made all the difference in how I view my enemies and myself.

↶

Help me to see my enemies with your eyes, Lord Jesus, and to follow your will instead of my own desires.

They Don't Know What They're Doing ∿

For in the way you judge, you will be judged; and by your standard of measure, it will be measured to you. Why do you look at the speck that is in your brother's eye, but do not notice the log that is in your own eye?

Matthew 7:2-3 (NAB)

When we're wrong about something — not when we realize it, but before that — we're like that coyote [in the roadrunner cartoons] after he's gone off the cliff and before he looks down. We're already wrong, we're already in trouble, but we feel like we're on solid ground. So I should actually correct something I said a moment ago. It *does* feel like something to be wrong. It feels like being right.

Kathryn Schulz, "On Being Wrong," TED Talk

∿

I am very often positively, absolutely, no-question-about-it right. Loudly and obnoxiously right. Oh, the embarrassment when I'm proven wrong. It turned out I "didn't know what I was doing."

I've been so grateful when people have been gracious about my mistakes and missteps, especially if we were in conflict. They've shown me Christ-like forgiveness. Can I do that for others when I'm the victim?

∿

Help me to remember to give people the benefit of the doubt when we disagree, for my own good as well as theirs.

GETTING TO HEAVEN

ↄ

In this a Christian consists,
that he gets rid of the earthly
and puts on the Heavenly man.

Pope St. Leo the Great

⌁ SPENDING TIME WITH GOD ⌁

Spending time with God is always transformative. But not every prayer leads to noticeable fruit.

James Martin, *The Abbey*

↵

True change takes time and work. I must be willing to be transformed, must strive to cooperate with God's work in me. I must also be patient.

↵

Show me, Lord Jesus. Draw me closer.

~ How Can You Get to Heaven

I always believed it was the things you don't choose that make you who you are. Your city, your neighborhood, your family. People here take pride in these things, like it was something they'd accomplished. The bodies around their souls, the cities wrapped around those. ... This city can be hard. When I was young, I asked my priest how you could get to heaven and still protect yourself from all the evil in the world. He told me what God said to His children. "You are sheep among wolves. Be wise as serpents, yet innocent as doves."

Patrick Kenzie, Gone Baby Gone film

~

Gone Baby Gone is a study in free will and trusting God. By the finale we realize that the entire story is an examination of those words: "You are sheep among wolves. Be wise as serpents, yet innocent as doves." We see who lives by them. Who doesn't. The price paid.

I realize this is how Jesus lived. Free will (wise as serpents). Trusting God (innocent as doves). He did it perfectly, of course.

That must be why Jesus spoke those words as instructions to the disciples when he sent them to proclaim the gospel to nearby villages. It was part of their training to be like him.

I suppose that means I must consider it part of my training. This seems mysterious and contradictory. How do I do it?

~

Lord, guide me. How can I live wise as a serpent, innocent as a dove?

And Be Safe from the World's Evils? ~

The human story does not always unfold like an arithmetical calculation on the principle that two and two make four. Sometimes in life they make five, or minus three, and sometimes the blackboard topples down in the middle of the sum and leaves the class in disorder and the pedagogue with a black eye. The element of the unexpected and the unforeseeable is what gives some of its relish to life, and saves us from falling into the mechanic thraldom of the logicians.

Winston Churchill, 1946, receiving the
Freedom of the City of Westminster

In all circumstances give thanks, for this is the will of God for you in Christ Jesus.

1 Thessalonians 5:18

~

I like things predictable and under control. There's no doubt the unexpected makes life more exciting. Sometimes in a good way, sometimes in a tragic way.

It's only when I remember to thank God for the bad as well as the good that I get proper perspective. It helps me to see the good that God may be bringing out of unexpected, upsetting events at that very moment.

Winston Churchill looked at life as a grand adventure. That's not my natural inclination but if I remember that the unexpected adds "relish" maybe my gratitude will give me that sense of adventure too.

~

Thank you, Lord, for all these things: the good, the bad, the unexpected.

⌁ The Problem is When We Don't

"Oh, of course. I'm wrong. Everything I say or do is wrong, according to you."

"But of course!" said the Spirit, shining with love and mirth so that my eyes were dazzled. "That's what we all find when we reach this country. We've all been wrong! That's the great joke. There's no need to go on pretending one was right! After that we begin living!

C. S. Lewis, *The Great Divorce*

⌁

To use the most basic language of the Bible, we are all sinners.

As someone once said to me, "God has already seen all that you do. Ignoring it means the only one you're fooling is yourself."

Sometimes I know it.

Sometimes it comes as a great shock. I really did fool myself! That moment of realization often makes me laugh at myself. And that's ok, as long as it doesn't make me hide my head in the sand, pretending I'm perfect.

⌁

Lord, I take myself so seriously. Help me to remember that my perspective isn't always right or as important as I think it is.

Let Ourselves Be Transformed ~

Since all have sinned and fall short of the glory of God, they are justified by his grace as a gift, through the redemption which is in Christ Jesus.

Romans 3:23-24 (RSV)

The problem is not in being sinners, the problem is when we don't let ourselves be transformed in love by the encounter with Christ.

Pope Francis, *Encountering Truth*

~

Yes. Recognizing my sin does me no good if I'm not willing to change, to let myself be changed by Christ.

~

Make me into the person I was created to be, dear Jesus.

❧ I Do Believe

"But if you can do anything, have compassion on us and help us."

And Jesus said to him, "'If you can!' All things are possible for one who believes."

Then the boy's father cried out, "I do believe, help my unbelief!"

Jesus, on seeing a crowd rapidly gathering, rebuked the unclean spirit and said to it, "Mute and deaf spirit, I command you: come out of him and never enter him again!"

Shouting and throwing the boy into convulsions, it came out. He became like a corpse, which caused many to say, "He is dead!"

But Jesus took him by the hand, raised him, and he stood up.

Mark 9:22-27 (NAB)

❧

I never noticed that "If you can!" from Jesus before.

It's not the reaction I expect from Jesus. No wonder the father instantly backs down: "I do believe, help my unbelief!" This is my cry too. Why am I tentative? When do I not believe? How am I turning away from what you would do for me?

❧

You can *do all things. Jesus, help my unbelief.*

HELP MY UNBELIEF ❧

Jesus said to him, "I will come and cure him."

The centurion said in reply, "Lord, I am not worthy to have you enter under my roof; only say the word and my servant will be healed. For I too am a person subject to authority, with soldiers subject to me. And I say to one, 'Go,' and he goes; and to another, 'Come here,' and he comes; and to my slave, 'Do this,' and he does it."

When Jesus heard this, he was amazed and said to those following him, "Amen, I say to you, in no one in Israel have I found such faith. [...]

And Jesus said to the centurion, "You may go; as you have believed, let it be done for you." And at that very hour [his] servant was healed.

Matthew 8: 7-10 (NAB)

❧

All I can think when I compare this story to the one on the opposite page is that Jesus heals both people. Belief or disbelief, he responds with healing.

The difference is that this healing is done from afar without a word, touch, or any external sign. As if by a thought, the servant is healed.

How much harder do I make things on myself when I limit what God would do for me?

❧

I do believe, Lord. Help my unbelief.

⤳ WHY ARE WE COWARDS ABOUT EVERYTHING

What is this, Lord, that we are cowards about everything except
being against you?

St. Teresa of Avila, Soliloquies 12

Every time we say "yes" to His will, God gives life.

Father James Yamauchi

⤳

I never thought before about how freely I sometimes turn my back
on what God asks. Especially when I know that God asks things of
me simply for my own good as well as that of others.

I'm ashamed to say how often I treat God like my servant instead
of my lord and savior.

⤳

*Lord, I want to put you first always. Remind me when I act like a
spoiled brat instead of your loving child.*

Except Being Against You? ∼

My God, how far am I from acting according to what I know so well! I confess it, my heart goes after shadows. I love anything better than communion with Thee. I am ever eager to get away from Thee. Often I find it difficult even to say my prayers. There is hardly any amusement I would not rather take up than set myself to think of Thee.

Give me grace, O my Father, to be utterly ashamed of my own reluctance! Rouse me from sloth and coldness, and make me desire Thee with my whole heart.

Blessed John Henry Newman, *Meditations and Devotions*

∼

I wish I didn't understand this so well.

∼

Shake me awake, dear Jesus. I cannot do this on my own.
I need you.

⌁ That Wasn't What We Had In Mind

The Chief Rabbi of London, Jonathan Sacks, wrote an op-ed for the London Times talking about using a GPS system in your car. The voice says, "go here, turn left, etc." He said the average Jewish male's response is "Who do you think I am? I'm going to turn right!"

When you do that, there's a sort of pause and after a while the voice says in effect, "Well, this wasn't what we had in mind, but since we're now here you probably want now to do this and this and this ..."

He said that is the story of the Children of Israel and God.
N. T. Wright, "Surprised by Scripture," Socrates in the City talk

⌁

Here we are again, still considering obedience and God's plan.

It's pretty easy to shake our heads at the Children of Israel. Clearly every time they ignored God's directions they wound up in a ditch crying for help.

I love the way God patiently tows them back to the right road and sets them up facing the right direction.

What I don't love is realizing that I am guilty of the same refusals, pride, and stupidity as the Children of Israel.

⌁

Lord, thank you for your patience. Please grant me the desire for obedience.

So You Need to Do This Instead ~

Do not quench the Spirit.

I Thessalonians 5:19

God's word is a command that brings with it the possibility of obeying. It creates its own "acceptable time." The hour rejected not only vanishes, but trails a wake of disaster.

Romano Guardini, The Lord

ᶜ

I've so often earned those trails of disaster that come when I reject God's word. Thank goodness for his restraint and tolerance under provocation.

I never thought about the fact that when I ignore God I am "quenching" the Holy Spirit. The word quench makes me think of thirst and rivers flowing, waterfalls pouring,

That's apt because Jesus spoke of the Spirit as "rivers of living water" (John 7:37–39). I shut the faucet on that river when I choose my own way. That's a vivid image. It hurts.

I have no one to blame but myself when that happens.

ᶜ

God, thank you for your patience and restraint! Thank you for second chances! May I obey promptly and let the Holy Spirit flow in my heart.

⁓ Unconfessed Sins are the Abyss

Going to confession is hard — hard when you have sins to confess and hard when you haven't, and you rack your brain for even the beginnings of sins against charity, chastity, sins of detraction, sloth or gluttony.

Dorothy Day, The Long Loneliness

"I suppose there are two views about everything," said Mark.

"Eh? Two views? There are a dozen views about everything until you know the answer. Then there's never more than one. But it's no affair of mine. Good night."

C. S. Lewis, That Hideous Strength

⁓

This is the beginning of letting myself be transformed by Christ's love. Honesty and self-knowledge about my failings is required so that I can begin to work toward the truth, toward being who I am meant to be.

⁓

Test me, O God, and know my thoughts.
See that my path is not wicked,
and lead me in the way everlasting.

see Psalm 139 (138): 23-24

Confessed Sins are the Bridge ～

To confess your sins to God is not to tell him anything he
doesn't already know. Until you confess them, however, they are
the abyss between you. When you confess them, they become
the Golden Gate bridge.

Frederick Buechner, *Wishful Thinking*

～

It is so freeing to make a clean breast of everything holding me
down. It's like pushing the restart button.

～

*Grant me the courage, Jesus, to fully repent and sincerely avoid
anything that would offend you.*

⌁ The Sin No Longer Exists

Consider all the past as nothing, and say, like David: Now I begin to love my God.

St. Francis de Sales

"I have sinned in thought, word, and deed, through my fault, through my fault, through my most grievous fault." But after you get done with it, don't go on brooding about it; don't keep thinking of it. You wipe your feet at the door of the church as you go in and you do not keep contemplating your dirty feet.

Dorothy Day, The Long Loneliness

↝

I've had those moments when I've dwelt upon sins that I've had forgiven. Seemingly I can't forgive myself. Does this make me more important than God? He forgives but I cannot? So that in itself is a sin I must fight.

In those moments, I've had a gentle wisp of thought appear, "Water under the bridge, Jules. Let it go."

If this is what he wants, who am I to disobey?

↝

Dear Jesus, help me to trust in your complete forgiveness.

NOW I BEGIN TO LOVE MY GOD ⁓

What do we mean when we say that "God forgives?" We certainly do not mean that he says: "Never mind. Try to do better in the future!" Or: "Don't worry, cheer up! I am not going to take it as seriously as all that." That would be quite unworthy, and the wrong would remain. We mean something far greater. We mean that the sin no longer exists in truth and reality and in the sight of my conscience.

Roman Guardini, *The Living God*

⁓

I know intellectually that the sin no longer exists. It is just that I forget to think of it that way.

I'm devaluing the importance of forgiveness and, therefore, the magnificence of what reconciliation with God really means — it brings me one step closer to who I was intended to be. And also, of course, one step closer to Him.

⁓

Thank you, God, for your great gift of cleansing and for drawing me closer to you.

⤳ LOVE YOUR ENEMIES

For if you love those who love you, what credit is that to you?
Even sinners love those who love them. ... But rather, love your
enemies and do good to them ...

Luke 6:32, 35

In loving your enemy, you want him to be your brother. ... What
he is as a human being is God's work; the hatred he bears towards you is his own work. And what do you say to yourself?
"Lord be kind to him, forgive his sins, inspire him with fear of
you, change him." In this person, you do not love what he is, but
what you want him to be. Thus when you love your enemy, you
love a brother.

St. Augustine, Homilies on the First Epistle of John

How do I show Christ-like forgiveness in real life? I can't control
the emotions that flood over me when I'm mad at someone. What I
can control is whether I wallow in them or ignore them and pray for
my enemy. I may have to do it a dozen times as the anger and hurt
pop up in my mind. Even if I don't "feel" love I can act on it
by praying.

That prayer will also help change me into the person I should
be. I can become who Jesus wants, a person who can love my
enemies and do good to them, right here, right now.

*Lord, have mercy on me and bless my enemy. I am not strong
enough to love him by myself. Help me to see with your eyes.*

AND DO GOOD TO THEM ~

Some say it is unreasonable to be courteous and gentle with a reckless person who insults you for no reason at all. I have made a pact with my tongue; not to speak when my heart is disturbed.

St. Francis de Sales

Shed light, not heat.

Ivereigh Austen, *How to Defend the Faith Without Raising Your Voice*

~

Holding my ton gue is one of the most difficult tasks I could set myself. I often must ask myself if speaking up will shed light or shed heat? It's surprising how helpful that simple question can be. It reminds me to put something first other than myself.

~

Thank you for the times I've remembered to ask myself that question and had the strength to keep the "pact with my tongue." Help me to do so always in difficult situations.

Finding Jesus in the Cross, the Resurrection, the Eucharist

Apart from the cross there is no other ladder by which we may get to heaven.

St. Rose of Lima

⌁ SPENDING TIME WITH GOD ⌁

Mary kept all these things, pondering them in her heart.

Luke 2:19 (RSV)

ꝯ

Pondering the mysteries of the cross, resurrection, and Eucharist is what helps bring my own life into focus.

ꝯ

When I feel I don't have time to sit and "do nothing" remind me, Lord Jesus, that this is what my life is for — to grow closer to you.

Litany of the Cross

The cross is the hope of Christians.
The cross is the resurrection of the dead.
The cross is the way of the lost.
The cross is the saviour of the lost.
The cross is the staff of the lame.
The cross is the guide of the blind.
The cross is the strength of the weak.
The cross is the doctor of the sick.
The cross is the aim of the priests.
The cross is the hope of the hopeless.
The cross is the freedom of the slaves.
The cross is the power of the kings.
The cross is the water of the seeds.
The cross is the consolation of the bondsmen.
The cross is the source of those who seek water.
The cross is the cloth of the naked.
We thank you, Father, for the cross.

Traditional

⸱

It seems odd to celebrate the cross this way. Then I remember why Jesus came and why he died. The cross was necessary.

The Church teaches that Christ saw each of us at every moment of his passion and death. He atoned for each of us individually as well as for mankind in general. He saw me. He saw you.

That's humbling. It makes the crucifixion personal. It really is because of me that he was nailed to the cross.

⸱

Meditate on the litany, applying each line to yourself. I was lame. I was blind. I was lost. I thank you, Father, for the cross!

Intended to Set Men Free ~

Says the Cross:
   Then the young Hero ungirt himself —
      that was God almighty,
   Strong, stiff-willed, and strode to the gallows,
   Climbed stout-hearted in the sight of many;
      intended to set men free.

The Dream of the Rood*

Sons of Gondor! Of Rohan! My brothers! I see in your eyes the same fear that would take the heart of me! A day may come when the courage of men fails, when we forsake our friends and break all bonds of fellowship. But it is not this day. An hour of wolves and shattered shields when the Age of Men comes crashing down. But it is not this day! This day we fight! By all that you hold dear on this good Earth, I bid you stand, Men of the West!

Aaragorn, The Return of the King film

~

I tend to think of Christ dreading his passion. However, the Anglo Saxons viewed Jesus as a warrior who didn't flinch and was even eager for the conflict that brought him to the destiny for which he was born.

Jesus himself said he "eagerly desired to eat this Passover with you." I don't forget Gethsemane. But I also can't forget that this is what he was born to do. Jesus was not weak but strong. He was eager to do the Father's will, out of love for him and love for us. I want to follow more closely in his footsteps.

~

Dear Lord Jesus, let me remember you came willingly and gladly for my redemption.

* Translated by Anthony Esolen

❧ Was Such a Great Thing as This

For ask now of the days that are past ... whether such a great thing as this has ever happened or was ever heard of. Did any people ever hear the voice of a god speaking out of the midst of the fire, as you have heard, and still live?

Or has any god ever attempted to go and take a nation for himself from the midst of another nation, by trials, by signs, by wonders, and by war, by a mighty hand and an outstretched arm, and by great terrors, according to all that the Lord your God did for you in Egypt before your eyes?

Deuteronomy 4:32-43 (RSV)

❧

Moses was speaking to the Hebrew people before he dies and they went to the land God promised them forty years before.

Of course, the answer is "no." No stories of gods in any lands have matched everything that God has done for them.

What has the Lord my God done before my eyes? Do I remember it? Does it help me to trust him? What will he yet bring me out of and move me towards?

❧

I thank you and praise you for all you have done for us.

Ever Heard Of? ～

Where can you run from His love?
Even the darkness cannot hide you.

Come Brothers Come
There is the sound of a rushing rain
To remove your sins and bind your wounds
You die for your god but our God died for us
The King of Kings comes to be the sacrificial lamb
Slain on the altar where we should have been

A Letter from the People of the Cross to ISIS

～

"You die for your god but our God died for us."

We are seeing history come alive as the first martyrs did, and with a message that should bring us all to our knees in gratitude and love. Jesus never stops, that's what we forget. He's in it with us, to the very end.

It suddenly hits home just how radical it is that God stepped into history so strongly, in person.

What has the Lord God done before our own eyes, right here, right now?

～

Thank you for pursuing me until I could ignore you no longer.
Come Lord Jesus.

⌁ DEATH SHALL BE NO MORE

Death, be not proud, though some have called thee
Mighty and dreadful, for thou art not so;
For those whom thou think'st thou dost overthrow
Die not, poor Death, nor yet canst thou kill me.
From rest and sleep, which but thy pictures be,
Much pleasure; then from thee much more must flow,
And soonest our best men with thee do go,
Rest of their bones, and soul's delivery.
Thou art slave to fate, chance, kings, and desperate men,
And dost with poison, war, and sickness dwell,
And poppy or charms can make us sleep as well
And better than thy stroke; why swell'st thou then?
One short sleep past, we wake eternally
And death shall be no more; Death, thou shalt die.

John Donne, Sonnet X

ↄ

Christ destroyed death.

I don't know why that never struck me with such force before.
Perhaps I've gone from thinking death is so far away from me to
being an age where it is disconcertingly possible. The reality of
death lurks in the back of my mind, waiting to pop up in the middle
of the night.

"We wake eternally and death shall be no more; Death, thou shalt
die." What reality and freedom those words bring.

ↄ

*Thank you, Jesus, for setting me free from death, in my worries
and in reality.*

DEATH, THOU SHALT DIE ᷜ

A guy asked me was I afraid. Of course I'm afraid. I've never died before.

Walter Payton not long before his death

No one has yet believed in God and the Kingdom of God, no one has yet heard about the realm of the resurrected, and not been homesick from that hour—waiting and looking forward to being released from bodily existence. ...

How do we know that dying is so dreadful? Who knows whether in our human fear and anguish, we are only shivering and shuddering at the most glorious, heavenly blessed event in the world?

Dietrich Bonhoeffer, 1933 sermon

ᷜ

I can't tell you how much I love Walter Payton's comment. Yes! That's why we are afraid. Death is a change so radical, into something so unknown, that naturally we fear it.

That's why Dietrich Bonhoeffer's reminder is so necessary. We know nothing personally about death. The one thing we know for sure is that Jesus, who loves each of us, is waiting on the other side of that door with new life.

Do I trust Him? That's what it comes down to.

ᷜ

Dying you destroyed my death, rising you restored my life. Lord Jesus, come in glory.

⌁ THE CROSS

"May I say," said Florence, "that you grieved to hear of the afflictions he has suffered?"

"Not," she replied, "if they [afflictions] have taught him that his daughter is very dear to him. He will not grieve for them himself, one day, if they have brought that lesson, Florence."

Charles Dickens, *Dombey and Son*

⌁

Florence's father went through incredible suffering, largely brought on by his very unrealistic view of his world and family. As he recovers, Florence strives for his reconciliation with her stepmother. That's when her stepmother points out that his afflictions were necessary for his redemption as a father.

This passage struck me dumb and redefined the book for me.

It is the mystery of the Cross in a nutshell.

Can I see past my own present trials to the great good that may be coming at this very moment because of them?

⌁

Jesus, help me to face my Cross with love and trust, just as you did. Show me the good that you bring from the midst of the bad.

IS A SIGN OF VICTORY ~

Satan tries to convince us that the Cross is a sign of failure; Our Lord Jesus Christ tells us it's a sign of victory. Facing and embracing our Cross is the way to our salvation — and that's why Satan hates it! That's why he tries to talk us out of it, because he doesn't want us to reach salvation.

Archbishop Timothy Dolan, *To Whom Shall We Go?*

We were promised sufferings. They were part of the program. We were even told, "Blessed are they that mourn," and I accept it. I've got nothing that I hadn't bargained for. Of course it is different when the thing happens to oneself, not to others, and in reality, not imagination.

C. S. Lewis, *A Grief Observed*

~

We follow a crucified Savior.

He understands when I want to avoid suffering. Even he had heartfelt prayers in the Garden of Gethsemane. But he knew there was a good that was greater than his personal desires. Do I know it myself?

In theory, and from past experience, I know that great good can come to me through the Cross. That is different from the present moment when I'm suffering. Then I have to fight self pity.

Sometimes suffering is inflicted by others. Sometimes I inflict it on myself as a natural consequence of my own actions. The question is do offer I it to God to do with as he will?

~

Don't let me forget the power of the Cross in my own life. Help me to remember to value it as Jesus did.

ᴗ Entirely Full of You

When I am completely united to you, there will be no more sorrow or trials; entirely full of you, my life will be complete.

St. Augustine*

ᴗ

If I am filled with God then there is no room for sorrow or trials. I will trust entirely. I will naturally want to do his will. How do I become completely united to God? The first step is being willing.

ᴗ

Fill me, Lord God.

* translation via *A Year with the Saints* by Paul Thigpen

My Life Will Be Complete ～

We must aim more and more to accomplish the divine will: not only desiring nothing special to happen to us, bad or even good, in this wretched life, thus keeping ourselves always at God's disposal, with heart and soul at peace. But we must also believe with a firm faith that Almighty God loves us more than we love ourselves, and takes more care of us than we could take of ourselves.

St. Catherine dei Ricci, letter to a nun

～

How do I let God fill me completely? St. Catherine shows the way. It is to desire nothing special, whether good or bad. That's difficult for me. I secretly hope for God to open up a parking space when traffic is bad.

But if I take things as God sends them, then I trust that what seems bad or good comes from one who knows the bigger picture about what I need.

This is how to be like Jesus, how to see the Cross as a sign of victory.

～

Jesus, help me to face my Cross with love and trust.

⌁ I Know the Resurrection

Never let anything so fill you with sorrow as to make you forget the joy of Christ risen.

St. Teresa of Calcutta, *Love: A Fruit Always in Season*

I know the resurrection is a fact, and Watergate proved it to me. How? Because 12 men testified they had seen Jesus raised from the dead, then they proclaimed that truth for 40 years, never once denying it. Every one was beaten, tortured, stoned and put in prison. They would not have endured that if it weren't true. Watergate embroiled 12 of the most powerful men in the world- and they couldn't keep a lie for three weeks. You're telling me 12 apostles could keep a lie for 40 years? Absolutely impossible.

Charles W. Colson, Easter Sunday 1982 speech

ع

This truth is so obvious once we have a clear example like Charles Colson gives. It never would have occurred to me to compare the apostles' example to how the Watergate conspirators couldn't stick to a lie. Everyone loves to tell a secret, after all.

The resurrection is true. It is what comes after the Cross ... and the cause of our joy.

ع

May my life be witness to the luminous joy of your resurrection, Lord Jesus.

Is a Fact ~

For me it is the virgin birth, the Incarnation, the resurrection which are the true laws of the flesh and the physical. Death, decay, destruction are the suspension of these laws. I am always astonished at the emphasis the Church puts on the body. It is not the soul she says that will rise but the body, glorified.

Flannery O'Connor, *The Habit of Being*

~

It is fascinating that the resurrection continues to teach us about Jesus. Not only in his words and presence, but when Jesus appears in a locked room, cooks and eats fish, walks with friends, lets them touch his wounds. He is there in the body, just not the sort we are used to. It is, as they say, "glorified."

It confirms the Incarnation as more than a convenient way for God to speak to us. It means our bodies are precious in a way that we don't think of in modern times.

~

Lord, may others recognize your love shining through all my words and actions.

⌁ God's New Project

Jesus's resurrection is the beginning of God's new project not to snatch people away from earth to heaven but to colonize earth with the life of heaven. That, after all, is what the Lord's Prayer is about.

N. T. Wright, *Surprised by Hope*

The Resurrection is not a single event, but a loosening of God's power and light into the earth and history that continues to alter all things, infusing them with the grace and power of God's own holiness. It is as though a door was opened, and what poured out will never be stopped, and that door cannot be closed.

Megan McKenna, *And Morning Came*

⌁

It sounds like science fiction: a door opening, flooding God's power into our time, colonizing earth with the life of heaven.

So often those sorts of stories have a hero striving to shut the door before something bad happens. In the true version of the story, our hero strives to open the door, sacrificing all and winning through to the happy ending of the resurrection.

This changes everything.

⌁

In your Resurrection, O Christ, let heaven and earth rejoice!"
Liturgy of the Hours

COLONIZE EARTH WITH THE LIFE OF HEAVEN ~

If anyone is in Christ, he is a new creation; the old has passed away, behold, the new has come.

2 Corinthians 5:17 (RSV)

But now the power of Easter has burst upon us with the resurrection of Christ. Now we find in ourselves a strength which is not our own, and which is freely given to us whenever we need it... Now we no longer strive to be good because we have to, because it is a duty, but because our joy is to please Him who has given all His love to us! Now our life is full of meaning!

Thomas Merton, Seasons of Celebration

~

I don't have to be afraid of death, or of not having love, or even of not being worthy. Christ went before me and came back to reassure me that he is with me. Truly this is joy.

~

Thank you for the hope and meaning that you have given to my life, Lord Jesus.

⌁ LO, I AM WITH YOU ALWAYS

I am the living bread that came down from heaven; whoever eats this bread will live forever; and the bread that I will give is my flesh for the life of the world.

John 6: 51

The Church draws her life from the Eucharist. This truth does not simply express a daily experience of faith, but recapitulates the heart of the mystery of the Church. In a variety of ways she joyfully experiences the constant fulfilment of the promise: "Lo, I am with you always, to the close of the age" (Matthew 28:20), but in the Holy Eucharist, through the changing of bread and wine into the body and blood of the Lord, she rejoices in this presence with unique intensity.

St. Pope John Paul II, Encyclical Ecclesia de Eucharistia*

↵

The Eucharist is the mystery which defines Catholicism. Do I recognize this core fact and express it with my own faith?

↵

Let me recognize You as Your disciples did at the breaking of the bread, so that the Eucharistic Communion be the Light which disperses the darkness, the force which sustains me, the unique joy of my heart.

St. Padre Pio's prayer

* Latin: The Church from the Eucharist

To the Close of the Age ∿

Out of the darkness of my life, so much frustrated, I put before you the one great thing to love on earth: the Blessed Sacrament … There you will find romance, glory, honour, fidelity, and the true way of all your loves upon earth.

J. R. R. Tolkien, *The Letters of J.R.R. Tolkien*

It became obvious why Catholics had built such beautiful cathedrals and churches throughout the world. Not as gathering or meeting places for Christians. But as a home for Jesus Himself in the Blessed Sacrament. Cathedrals house Jesus. Christians merely come and visit Him. The cathedrals and churches architecturally prepare our souls for the beauty of the Eucharist.

Allen R. Hunt, *Confessions of a Mega Church Pastor*

∿

Do I let my church's beauty prepare my soul for the beauty of the Eucharist? For the romance, glory, and love I will find there?

∿

I adore You, O Christ, present here and in all the churches of the world, for by Your holy cross You have redeemed the world.
St. Francis of Assisi's prayer

⤳ "Well, If It's a Symbol

Whoever eats my flesh and drinks my blood has eternal life, and I will raise him on the last day. For my flesh is true food, and my blood is true drink. Whoever eats my flesh and drinks my blood remains in me and I in him.

Many of his disciples, when they heard it, said, "This is a hard saying; who can listen to it?"

After this many of his disciples drew back and no longer went about with him.

Jesus said to the twelve, "Do you also wish to go away?" Simon Peter answered him, "Lord, to whom shall we go? You have the words of eternal life; and we have believed, and have come to know, that you are the Holy One of God."

John 6:54-56, 60, 66-69

⤴

Do I "understand" the Eucharist? No.

Do I believe it is the body and blood, soul and divinity of Jesus Christ? Yes.

Like Peter, I don't have to understand it in order to trust Jesus.

⤴

I adore You, O Christ, present here and in all the churches of the world, for by Your holy cross You have redeemed the world.
St. Francis of Assisi's prayer

THEN TO HELL WITH IT" ∽

Toward morning the conversation turned on the Eucharist, which I, being the Catholic, was obviously supposed to defend. Mrs. Broadwater said when she was a child and received the Host, she thought of it as the Holy Ghost, He being the "most portable" person of the Trinity; now she thought of it as a symbol and implied that it was a pretty good one. I then said, in a very shaky voice, "Well, if it's a symbol, to hell with it." That was all the defense I was capable of but I realize now that this is all I will ever be able to say about it, outside of a story, except that it is the center of existence for me; all the rest of life is expendable.

Flannery O'Connor, *The Habit of Being*

∽

The further I grow in my Catholic life, the more it sinks in that the Eucharist is the one non-negotiable. Jesus is truly present and no symbol.

If this is a troublesome point, spend time reading chapter six of the Gospel of John, while asking Jesus to answer your questions or doubts.

∽

O Jesus in the Blessed Sacrament, I would like to be filled with love for You; keep me closely united with You, may my heart be near to Yours.

St. Pope John XXIII's prayer

Becoming holy

~

Jesus, help me to simplify my life
by learning what you want me to be —
and becoming that person.

St. Thérèse of Lisieux, Story of a Soul

❧ BEAR CHRIST INTO THE WORLD ❧

He said to them in reply, "My mother and my brothers are those who hear the word of God and act on it."

Luke 8:21

Mary's perfect obedience makes her the perfect disciple. She willingly bore Christ into the world. What makes us disciples? We should also bear the Word into the world.

Father John Libone, homily

ᴄ

How do I bear the Word into the world? I do it in my attempts to be obedient, which bring me closer to holiness.

ᴄ

My soul magnifies the Lord,
and my spirit rejoices in God my Savior.

From Mary's Magnificat, Luke 1:46-47

❧ "How Do You Expect to Become a Saint?"

"I can't be a saint," I said, "I can't be a saint." And my mind darkened with a confusion of realities and unrealities: the knowledge of my own sins, and the false humility which makes men say that they cannot do the things that they must do, cannot reach the level that they must reach: the cowardice that says: "I am satisfied to save my soul, to keep out of mortal sin," but which means, by those words: "I do not want to give up my sins and my attachments."

Lax said: "All that is necessary to be a saint is to want to be one. Don't you believe that God will make you what He created you to be, if you will consent to let him do it? All you have to do is desire it."

Thomas Merton, The Seven Storey Mountain

God would never inspire me with desires which cannot be realized; so in spite of my littleness, I can hope to be a saint.

St. Thérèse of Lisieux, Story of a Soul

❧

That passage from Merton changed my life. It gave me a look at the higher purpose for which I was born, for which we all were born. I have the same doubts that Merton did, but I also know that God can do all things if we will let him.

And then when I read Saint Thérèse, I realize my desire is itself a reason to hope.

❧

God, I want to be a saint. Make my heart like yours.

"By Wanting To" ~

One might say that the saints are, so to speak, new Christian constellations, in which the richness of God's goodness is reflected. Their light, coming from God, enables us to know better the interior richness of God's great light.

Pope Benedict XVI, *The Spirit of the Liturgy*

It is part of the Roman Catholic idea of the saints that each mirrors Christ in an individual way, expressing facets of the infinite Personality, which could not all be expressed in one finite life, no matter how great. The historical Christ, for example, was not a philosopher nor a king; but St. Thomas Aquinas and St. Louis of France show us something of what He might have been like if He had been.

Richard Purtill, *Elves and Eldils*

ↄ

Saints inspire me by reflecting some aspect of God's goodness, like the moon reflects the sun. They help me to see how to live the way Jesus would want.

I want to be a saint, so that applies to me too. What about God do I mirror? Can I see Christ in myself, in my actions and words? Does my life show him to others?

ↄ

Jesus, help me to become my best self so I may bring others to you.

ᵔ IF HE CALLED ME TO DO IT

Fear thou not; for I am with thee: be not dismayed; for I am thy God: I will strengthen thee; yea, I will help thee; yea, I will uphold thee with the right hand of my righteousness.

Isaiah 41:10 (KJV)

My whole life had been one of keeping out of public duties, but the leading of Christ seemed now to be in the opposite direction, and I shrank from going forward. At this time I decided to put it all on Christ—after all if He called me to do it, then He would have to supply the necessary power. In going forward the power was given me.

*Eric Liddell

ᵔ

I was in a similar circumstance of being led in a way I usually avoided. I also found myself shrinking from going forward. Eric Liddell's quote, who underwent greater challenges than I am ever likely to, reminds me that I am not alone.

When I read this, I felt a great sense of relief, as if a great weight had literally just been lifted from my shoulders. My job is to be faithful. The "power" is not my worry.

ᵔ

Thank you, Lord, for being faithful to your promises. And for supplying the power to do your will.

* quoted in *Eric Liddell: Pure Gold* by David McCasland

Eric Liddell was the Olympic runner who refused to compete on Sunday, whose story was told in the movie *Chariots of Fire*. What is little known is that after ten years in China as a missionary, he was imprisoned for two years in a Japanese prison camp during WWII. He had a chance to leave but gave his place to a pregnant woman. He died just months before the camp was liberated.

He Would Have to Supply the Power ❧

We know that all things work for good for those who love God,
who are called according to his purpose.

Romans 8:28

Lord, if this is what this is all about, then I thank you. I praise
you for leaving me in prison, for letting them take away my li-
cense to practice law, yes, even for my son being arrested. I praise
you for giving me your love through these men, for being God,
for just letting me walk with Jesus.

Chuck Colson's prayer of surrender to God's will, Born Again

❧

This makes me think of The Hiding Place when Betsy ten Boom
tells her sister Corrie that everything in our past happened to
prepare us for what is happening right now.

That requires a greater trust in God's plan than many of us
have. Certainly it strains my belief sometimes. But even the bad
circumstances of our lives will be used by God to bring great good
we cannot imagine.

Do I trust God enough to thank him for every circumstance, even
when it seems bad, even when I can't see why it happened?

❧

Help me to trust your purpose through all things.

⌁ Like a Tree Planted by Water

Like a stream is the king's heart in the hand of the Lord; wherever it pleases him, he directs it.

Proverbs 21:1 (NAB)

Blessed is the man who trusts in the Lord,
  whose hope is in the Lord.
He is like a tree planted beside the waters
  that stretches out its roots to the stream:
It fears not the heat when it comes,
  its leaves stay green;
In the year of drought it shows not distress,
  but still bears fruit.

Jeremiah 17:7-8 (NAB)

↝

That tree is a powerful image of trust. I was particularly impressed when I noticed that we are not told it will be protected from everything—the year of drought will come.

But in that drought it will still bear fruit.

↝

Lord, direct my heart so that my roots go deep and I am not anxious in drought.

Not Anxious in the Drought ~

Look at the birds in the sky; they do not sow or reap, they gather nothing into barns, yet your heavenly Father feeds them. Are not you more important than they? Can any of you by worrying add a single moment to your life-span?

Matthew 6:26-27

~

When I stop and think about it, I really control so little in my life.

I suppose that is one of the things that Jesus' own life illustrated. He lived by the lessons he taught.

I need to remember that God truly holds me in his hands.

~

Good Jesus, in you alone have I placed all my trust. You are my strength and my only refuge; I give and abandon myself entirely to you. Do with me whatever you please.

A Prayer of St. John Eudes

⤳ Jesus' Message is What Counts

That Jesus' task "is consummated" must be true, because he says so (John 19:30). Yet what a spectacle of failure! His word rejected, his message misunderstood, his commands ignored. None the less, his appointed task is accomplished, through obedience to the death—that obedience whose purity counterbalances the sins of a world. That Jesus delivered his message is what counts— not the world's reaction; and once proclaimed, that message can never be silenced, but will knock on men's hearts to the last day.

Romano Guardini, *The Lord*

ↄ

When you know the difference that Christ has made in your life, there is a sort of delight in the perversity of considering Jesus a "spectacle of failure."

When has standard success healed the deepest hurts of the soul, restored joy and hope, and given a trustworthy promise of eternal life with God forever?

ↄ

Jesus, every good thing that makes my life worth living is a gift you gave me. I can never thank you enough.

SHOW ME YOUR WAY, O LORD ~

Most High, glorious God,
enlighten the darkness of my heart
and give me true faith, certain hope, and perfect charity,
sense, and knowledge, Lord,
that I may carry out Your holy and true command.
Amen.

St. Francis of Assisi, prayer in front of the crucifix

~

St. Francis used to pray this in front of the crucifix while he was
discerning his vocation. We can see from that just how dangerous
the prayer is. We might become saints.

That means, of course, that it is a hopeful prayer because to be
a saint is to fulfill your heart's dearest desire, the thing we were
created to do. It might not be easy but it will turn out to be the most
satisfying thing you've ever done.

We just don't know what it is until we follow that path.

~

Speak, Lord, your servant is listening.

⌁ LOVE ONE ANOTHER

This is my commandment: love one another as I love you.

John 15:12

Here at least is the last and deepest lesson of Charles Dickens. ...
Every day we are missing a monster whom we might easily love
and an imbecile whom we should certainly admire. This is the
real gospel of Dickens; the inexhaustible opportunities offered
by the liberty and variety of man.

G. K. Chesterton, Charles Dickens

⌁

Jesus' message is one that he died to deliver. He told his disciples
to "love one another" just before going to his passion, crucifixion,
and resurrection.

That tells me how important it was, how key, how central. What do
I do with that commandment? Do I obey it or ignore it?

⌁

*Love comes from you, Lord. Help me to live your commandment
with my whole heart.*

As I Have Loved You ⌁

"Do you think people are doing the best they can?" [...]

Steve said, "I don't know. I really don't. All I know is that my life is better when I assume that people are doing their best. It keeps me out of judgment and lets me focus on what is, and not what should or could be." His answer felt like truth to me. Not an easy truth, but truth.

Brené Brown, Rising Strong

I would prefer to combat the "I'm special" feeling not by the thought "I'm no more special than anyone else" but by the feeling "Everyone is as special as me." ... The first might lead you to think, "I'm only one of the crowd like everyone else." But the second leads to the truth that there isn't any crowd. No one is like anyone else.

C. S. Lewis, 1952 letter

⌁

When I can remember to assume people are doing their best, it does bring out the best in me. The problem is that I often don't remember to make that assumption. How do I live that truth more consistently? Perhaps by keeping in mind, "Everyone is as special as me."

⌁

Remind me, Lord, touch my heart.

↭ Someone Else's Idea

Do you ever wonder why God values obedience more than sacrifice? ... Because obedience is someone else's idea of what you should sacrifice.

David Manuel

We have nothing of our own but our will. It is the only thing that God has so placed in our own power that we can make an offering of it to him.

St. John Vianney

ↄ

Why am I surprised every time I realize that *being* obedient is hard in a way that thinking about it never is.

Jesus was obedient because he so perfectly identified with God the Father's will. I realize how far I am from choosing the Father's will over my own. I guess that's a sign of how far I am from fully following Jesus.

ↄ

Receive, O Lord, all my liberty.
Take my memory, my understanding,
and my entire will.
Whatsoever I have or hold,
You have given me.

I give it all back to You
and surrender it wholly
to be governed by your will.

Give me only your love and your grace,
and I am rich enough
and ask for nothing more.

Sucipe prayer, "Receive," St. Ignatius of Loyola

OF WHAT YOU SHOULD SACRIFICE ~

I often thought my constitution would never endure the work I had to do, (but) the Lord said to me: "Daughter, obedience gives strength."

St. Teresa of Avila, Foundations

Don't say, "That's the way I am — it's my character." It's your *lack* of character.

St. Josemaria Escriva, The Way

~

This is heartening in a way. Knowing the truth about myself means I'm not believing my own excuses or lies. It gives me a solid place to begin again.

I often listen to my feelings and do what I want when what I really ought to do is my duty. Ultimately that would leave me happier, with fewer regrets. And perhaps it would build some of that character which I lack.

~

Dearest Lord, strengthen me. Help me see my weak spots and have the will to avoid them.

◦ THAT OTHERS MAY BECOME HOLIER THAN I

O Jesus! Meek and humble of heart, *Hear me.*
   From the desire of being esteemed,
   Deliver me, Jesus.

From the desire of being loved ... *Deliver me, Jesus.*
From the desire of being extolled ... *Deliver me, Jesus.*
From the desire of being honored ... *Deliver me, Jesus.*
From the desire of being praised ... *Deliver me, Jesus.*
From the desire of being preferred to others ... *Deliver me, Jesus.*
From the desire of being consulted ... *Deliver me, Jesus.*
From the desire of being approved ... *Deliver me, Jesus.*
From the fear of being humiliated ... *Deliver me, Jesus.*
From the fear of being despised ... *Deliver me, Jesus.*
From the fear of suffering rebukes ... *Deliver me, Jesus.*
From the fear of being calumniated* ... *Deliver me, Jesus.*
From the fear of being forgotten ... *Deliver me, Jesus.*
From the fear of being ridiculed ... *Deliver me, Jesus.*
From the fear of being wronged ... *Deliver me, Jesus.*
From the fear of being suspected ... *Deliver me, Jesus.*

That others may be loved more than I,
   Jesus, grant me the grace to desire it.

That others may be esteemed more than I ...
   Jesus, grant me the grace to desire it.
That, in the opinion of the world, others may increase and I may
   decrease ... *Jesus, grant me the grace to desire it.*
That others may be chosen and I set aside ...
   Jesus, grant me the grace to desire it.

(continued on next page)

Provided I Become as Holy as I Should ~

That others may be praised and I unnoticed ...
Jesus, grant me the grace to desire it.
That others may be preferred to me in everything ...
Jesus, grant me the grace to desire it.
That others may become holier than I, provided that I may
become as holy as I should ...
Jesus, grant me the grace to desire it.

Traditional

~

I like litanies. I know they're considered very old fashioned. A litany like this, about humility, raises eyebrows. I've been told it turns people off to pray about humility.

Maybe.

After all humility is about knowing who you are, who God is, and where your relationship with him is right or wrong. What's so bad about that? If I never look at where I might be wrong, how will I know what to make right?

Everything in the litany is from Jesus' life. He did the Father's will without desiring, fearing, or wanting others' esteem. They seem impossible for me, but all things are possible with God.

I want to be transformed by love so that God can do the impossible, both for me and through me. For that I need to know where I stand. Let's begin.

~

Pray the litany aloud, thinking about Jesus' example for each item. Holy Spirit, guide my mind and open my heart to hear what you want to teach me.

* To utter maliciously false statements

✢ Ask the Beasts

Ask the beasts, and they will teach you;
    the birds of the air, and they will tell you;
or the plants of the earth, and they will teach you;
    and the fish of the sea will declare to you.
Who among all these does not know
    that the hand of the Lord has done this?
In his hand is the life of every living thing
    and the breath of all mankind.

Job 11:7-10 (RSV)

Outside the moon had come out. It was full, a disk of bright silver. I saw a large, dramatic spider web on my back porch that must have been made while I was in the house with my mind in turmoil; the spider was just finishing the outer circle of it. The moon illuminated the strands of the big taut web so that it seemed to be made of pure light. It was dazzling, geometric and mysterious, and it calmed me just to stop and look at it, at the elaboration and power of life that could make such a design.

Walter Tevis, Mockingbird

ꙅ

I love nature as "other" and also something I'm part of. Wordless lessons are imparted to me by it. They are lessons I can't always verbalize myself.

What does nature show me of "the hand of the Lord?" How does it draw me closer to him?

ꙅ

Thank you for speaking even when there are no words.

And They Will Teach You ~

One July evening, cloudless, moonless, with just a hint of a humid breeze, her father took her out into the back yard in the dark and told her to look up at the sky.

From one horizon to the other, all across the black carpet of the night, were the stars — thousands of them, tens of thousands, in clusters and rivers of light. And in the quiet, her father said, "God made the world beautiful because he loves us."

That was more than sixty years ago. ... still, when she closes her eyes, she can see that carpet of stars and hear her father's voice: *God made the world beautiful because he loves us.* Creation is more than an accident of dead matter. It's a romance. It has purpose. It sings of the Living God. It bears his signature. And it's our home.

Charles J. Chaput, *Strangers in a Strange Land*

ↄ

Seeing the world's beauty as God's loving gift warms me. Whatever I am struggling with matters less.

I look out my window: clouds flowing before the wind, tender spring leaves, a cheeky robin, my crazy dog — all signs of a great, tender love who wanted me surrounded by beauty and wonder. This speaks to the deepest parts of my heart. It says so much about who Jesus is and how much he loves us.

It really is a romance.

ↄ

Lord, thank you for the beauty and love I see in creation.

⌁ THE MIRACLE REVEALS THE WORLD

The miracle reveals the world as it appears to God ... [Miracles] are given to us to strengthen our faith, to suggest to us how things really stand with the world, only that we have not the eyes to see and must take Christ at his word. God looks upon every one of us as he looked at the widow behind the bier. [Luke 7:11-17]

Romano Guardini, *The Lord*

⸱

I see God in the world, in nature. But there have been occasions when God has given me a bigger sign about himself. What I have experienced makes me think that miracles might be more common than most of us realize. After all, I'm not particularly important or special ... or even good.

Every single one spoke a single truth: God loves us, loves me, more than I can possibly imagine.

And that's divine reality.

⸱

Dearest Jesus, thank you for those glimpses of divine reality.
Thank you for loving me.

AS IT APPEARS TO GOD ~

The miracles of the church seem to me to rest not so much upon faces or voices or healing power coming suddenly near to us from afar off, but upon our perceptions being made finer, so that for a moment our eyes can see and our ears can hear what is there about us always.

Willa Cather, Death Comes for the Archbishop

By freeing some individuals from the earthly evils of hunger, injustice, illness and death, Jesus performed messianic signs. Nevertheless he did not come to abolish all evils here below, but to free men from the gravest slavery, sin, which thwarts them in their vocation as God's sons and causes all forms of human bondage.

Catechism of the Catholic Church, 549

~

If miracles show us how God sees the world then think how much I'm missing all the time. That means sin, something else that is often invisible to me, is absolutely deadly. It is what Jesus came to free us from.

Why does that so easily slip my mind? Why does it take a miracle to wake me up?

And yet our freedom, our salvation, is so important to Jesus that he came in person and sacrificed himself.

That is divine reality. That is true love.

~

I praise you and thank you, Jesus, for your miracles and your sacrifice. Help me to be worthy.

WAYS TO PRAY

You, Lord, are near to all who call upon you,
to all who call upon you in truth.

Psalm 145:18 *(NAB)*

◌ LIFE IS A CHALLENGE TO PRAYER ◌

Progress and success, care and distress, illness and recovery, birth and death: everything that happens in life must find expression in prayer and determine its nature. We must become more sensitive and perhaps — if we may put it thus — more inventive. Prayer should not always be restricted to the selfsame thoughts and words while life passes by in all its diversity.

Romano Guardini, The Art of Praying

ﭒ

I talk to people differently depending on our relationship, what's happening in my life, and a hundred other variables. Why would talking to God be any different? He is always the same but I am not.

ﭒ

My life is always changing, but you, Lord, are always the one I long for. Draw me closer. Help me to find you.

⌁ A Mere Breath

The reality of God can make itself felt as a mere breath or the mighty flood which completely fills man. It is experienced in our innermost soul, by the loftiest heights of our spirit and by all that is most pure in our being. It is unique and simple and yet possesses the most diverse properties.

Romano Guardini, *The Art of Praying*

⌁

I, naturally, often have trouble knowing how best to connect with God. I do know that putting myself in God's presence is key. And the same thing doesn't always work from week to week, or even from day to day. He's always waiting but I'm not always paying attention in the right way.

I'm glad the Church has so many different approaches to help me open my heart and mind. A few of my favorites are included in this section.

⌁

Lord, you know my innermost heart. Help me to know how best to seek your presence.

OR A MIGHTY FLOOD ⁓

God speaks to souls through words uttered by pious people, by sermons or good books, and in many other such ways. Sometimes he calls souls by means of sickness or troubles, or by some truth He teaches them during prayer, for tepid as they may be in seeking Him, yet God holds them very dear.

Teresa of Avila, The Interior Castle

And he said, "Go forth, and stand upon the mount before the Lord." And behold, the Lord passed by, and a great and strong wind rent the mountains, and broke in pieces the rocks before the Lord, but the Lord was not in the wind; and after the wind an earthquake, but the Lord was not in the earthquake; and after the earthquake a fire, but the Lord was not in the fire; and after the fire a still small voice. And when Elijah heard it, he wrapped his face in his mantle and went out and stood at the entrance of the cave. And behold, there came a voice to him, and said, "What are you doing here, Elijah?"

1 Kings 19:11-13 (RSV)

⁓

God himself speaks to me in different ways at different times. He knows what will reach me best depending on my mood, frame of mind, emotional state, or even location.

The question is, does the Lord have to hit me with an earthquake to get my attention? No matter how I am praying, am I also listening? Am I open to hear His voice?

⁓

May I always be open to hear your voice.

᪲ Kneeling

... prayer has one of its typical expressions in the gesture of kneeling. It is a gesture that has in itself a radical ambivalence. In fact, I can be forced to kneel — a condition of indigence and slavery — but I can also kneel spontaneously, declaring my limitations and therefore my being in need of Another. To him I declare I am weak, needy, "a sinner."

Pope Benedict XVI, Prayer

᪲

Not long ago I found myself feeling I should kneel when I prayed. As an adult convert, I'd been taught that prayer "works" in any position one wants so I usually sat for prayer. This inner urge seemed odd but it was insistent so I tried it.

Kneeling felt right somehow. I was focused on what I was doing. It was harder for my mind drift into my own thoughts. The time I spent kneeling grew longer and longer. I don't do it every day but kneeling has become a cherished part of my prayer life.

᪲

Dearest Jesus, whether on my knees or not, may I always know I am in need of you.

WITH A TIMER ~

For many years I kept wishing the time would be over. I had more in mind the clock striking twelve than other good things. Often I would have preferred some serious penance to becoming recollected in prayer.

Teresa of Avila, *Autobiography*

~

One of my essential prayer tools is a kitchen timer. I set it to the ideal time, turn the face away, and then begin fighting the urge to turn it around to see how much time I've got left.

On good days it allows me to relax and become recollected in God's presence. On bad days, the best I might achieve is continually pulling my mind away from the temptation to see how much time is left. That struggle in itself can be a sort of prayer. If it's the best I can do, then that is what I offer to God.

~

Grant me the strength and love to keep you at the center of my life, Lord. Most of all I greatly desire to give our conversations the attention they deserve.

ᵛ I Offer You

Lord, open my lips
And my mouth shall proclaim your praise.

Morning Prayer, Liturgy of the Hours

Cry out with joy to the Lord, all the earth.
Serve the Lord with gladness.
Come before him, singing for joy.
Come, let us worship God who brings the world and its
   wonders from darkness into light.

Psalm 100, Morning Prayer, Liturgy of the Hours

ᵕ

The Morning Offering begins your day by putting yourself and
everything you may encounter into God's hands. There are
different versions of the prayer and I've had various people press
them on me as being absolutely necessary.

It never interested me until, oddly enough, I realized that I was
saying my own Morning Offering almost as an insurance policy. I'd
have mornings when I'd forget to pray any of my favorite prayers,
many of which have been mentioned on previous pages. I felt
adrift and soon fell into the habit of casting myself and the day into
God's hands with a simple, all-inclusive prayer. It becomes my
anchor for the rest of the day.

ᵕ

*Lord, I offer you my day, with all the joys and sorrows I
encounter. Use it for your glory. Amen.*

My Day ～

Caprice capocuoco. Your Morning Offering and evening Examen* are the pizza dough. God scatters the savory bits through your day at his discretion.

Father John Libone

～

Caprice capocuoco means chef's caprice or whimsy. In Italy, Father told me, when you go to a pizza place and ask for *caprice capocuoco* you get whatever strikes the chef at that moment. It may be very similar to other things on the menu but the proportions or sizes will be unique to your piece.

I really love the mental image of God expertly scattering various events and encounters through my day, giving it the special twist that makes it mine alone. It makes me excited and curious about the day to come. (C'mon pepperoni!) It gives me something to ponder even at the end of a bad day. (Darn. Anchovies again!)

～

I trust you with the day ahead, Jesus. Caprice capouoco *please!*

* Examen is discussed on pages 162-163.

⌁ Establishing a Regular

Establishing a regular schedule for prayer ... Above all, it consists in saying one's prayers at certain fixed hours: in the morning before starting the tasks of the day and in the evening before retiring. In addition everyone should do what he thinks right, what he is able to do and what suits his routine. ...

Whatever routine one may adopt, one should carry it out honestly and conscientiously. In matters of prayer we are only too apt to deceive ourselves because, generally speaking, man does not enjoy praying. ... Better to say openly, "I do not wish to pray," than to make excuses.

Romano Guardini, The Art of Praying

↝

In addition to touching base in the morning and evening, I also use mealtime prayers as a chance to gather myself a little more consciously. "Bless us, O Lord, and these Thy gifts" never fails to make me think of the other people at the table or just remind me that I haven't thought of God since the last time I prayed.

Those little prayer bombs jolt me back to awareness of God but that's not enough. I have to schedule time in my day for a longer conversation. That's the one that is tough to make myself do.

Why? I'm selfish with my time. Think about your obstacles to prayer and what lie at the bottom of them. And then just do it anyway. Spend at least 10 minutes talking to God today and every day.

↝

Lord, help me win the struggle to devote myself to prayer, being watchful and thankful.

see Colossians 4:2

Schedule for Prayer ~

Glorious Saint _____, my beloved patron, you served God in humility and with confidence on earth. Now you enjoy his beatific vision in heaven. You persevered until death and gained the crown of eternal life. Remember now the dangers and confusion and anguish that surround me in my needs and troubles, especially:

(Mention your request)

Amen.

Traditional novena

~

This has become part of my daily morning prayer. It is short and pithy. Most of all, it connects me with my patron saint, forcing me to slow down for a couple of minutes and consider her life, how she loved and served God, and the help she can give me this day.

I have a lot of concrete examples to consider because my patron is Saint Martha (Luke 10:38-42, John 11:1-53, John 12:1-9) who was a personal friend of Jesus. But every time I say this prayer, a different example pops to mind of her perseverance, loyalty, service, and love. And of how those connect with my life right now.

Your patron has just as many examples for you. They are waiting to help us. All we have to do is ask.

~

Lord thank you for my patron saint, a divinely inspired match with the best friend, the best "example," to help me get to heaven.

"Are we going now, Don Camillo?" asked Christ from above the altar. "The river must be beautiful in this sunshine. I'll enjoy seeing it."

"We're going all right," replied Don Camillo. "But I am afraid that this time I shall be the entire procession. If You can put up with that..."

"Where there is Don Camillo he is sufficient in himself," said Christ smiling.

Don Camillo hastily put on the leather harness with the support for the foot of the cross, lifted the enormous crucifix from the altar and adjusted it in the socket. Then he sighed: "All the same, they need not have made this Cross quite so heavy."

"You're telling Me!" replied the Lord smiling. "And I never had shoulders such as yours."

Giovanni Guareschi, *The Little World of Don Camillo*

᠄

This is the example I keep before me when I've been feeling a bit distant from the Lord. It reminds me that I need to talk to Jesus about my everyday life. I imagine Don Camillo's Christ on the cross chatting with me and suddenly I am sharing the most mundane cares, fears, jokes, and hopes of my day.

᠄

Thank you for the examples that remind me you're ready for a casual chat just as much as helping with the big issues.

AS TO YOUR DEAREST FRIEND* ~

On a long and arduous journey St. Teresa of Avila was dumped
into a large mud puddle. She heard God saying, "This is how I
treat my friends, Teresa," She answered, "No wonder you have so
few of them, Lord!"

My version of a much told story

Martha, burdened with much serving, came to him and said,
"Lord, do you not care that my sister has left me by myself to do
the serving? Tell her to help me."

Luke 10:40

And Peter took him and began to rebuke him, saying, "God for-
bid, Lord! This shall never happen to you." But he turned and
said to Peter, "Get behind me, Satan! You are a hindrance to me;
for you are not on the side of God, but of men."

Matthew 16: 22-23 (RSV)

Jesus said, "Take away the stone." Martha, the dead man's sister,
said to him, "Lord, by now there will be a stench; he has been
dead for four days."

John 11:39

~

They joke, complain, argue, and blurt out their feelings. This
is plain speaking from confident friends. That free and easy
exchange is one you can only have with someone you know
really well. I want to have such natural conversations. And when I
remember these examples, I do.

~

*Dear Jesus, help me to remember that plain talk is often the best
talk — when it is from the heart.*

* St. Alphonsus de Liguori, full quote on page 8.

ᙚ THIS ENDLESS VARIETY GREATLY ENHANCES

The order of God's Providence maintains a perpetual vicissitude in the material being of this world; day is continually turning to night, spring to summer, summer to autumn, autumn to winter, winter to spring; no two days are ever exactly alike. Some are foggy, rainy, some dry or windy; and this endless variety greatly enhances the beauty of the universe. And even so precisely is it with man (who, as ancient writers have said, is a miniature of the world), for he is never long in any one condition, and his life on earth flows by like the mighty waters, heaving and tossing with an endless variety of motion; one while raising him on high with hope, another plunging him low in fear; now turning him to the right with rejoicing, then driving him to the left with sorrows; and no single day, no, not even one hour, is entirely the same as any other of his life.

St. Francis de Sales, *Introduction to the Devout Life*

ᕈ

I launch into the day, only to find it is nothing like I expected. Even when it is like I expected, for better or worse, I'm thrown for a loop by little details.

I forget how many variables make every day different from the one before it. How right St. Francis de Sales was: "This endless variety greatly enhances the beauty of the universe." The endless variety of my life, whether good or bad, enhances the beauty of my life.

The challenge of every day is to remember it.

ᕈ

Dear Lord, you never change. Whether today is a high or a low, happy or sad, help me to keep my eyes on you.

THE BEAUTY OF OUR DAILY LIVES ~

From the universe we learn that God is infinite, that we cannot compass him at all. From such things as insects, flies, little frogs, mice and flowers, we learn that to us he is something else. He is Father, brother, child, and friend.

If you have ever had a little green tree frog and watched him puffing out with a pomposity worthy of a dragon before croaking, you must have guessed that there is a tender smile on our Heavenly Father's face, that he likes us to laugh and laughs with us; the frog will teach your heart more than all the books of theology in your world.

Caryll Houselander, *Mother of Christ*

~

This is why I have to pay attention to that "endless variety." What waits for me in the world around me, in the people I encounter, in all the little highs and lows of each day? I begin each day determined to keep my eyes open.

~

Show me, Lord, yourself in this day. Help me to be present in the moment.

⤙ WHERE WAS GOD

Examine yourselves, to see whether you are holding to your faith. Test yourselves. Do you not realize that Jesus Christ is in you? — unless indeed you fail to meet the test!

2 Corinthians 13:5 (RSV)

Think of it as a movie playing in your head. Push the play button and run through your day, from start to finish ... sights, sounds, feelings, tastes, textures, conversations. ... Each moment offers a window to where God has been in your day.

James Martin, *The Jesuit Guide to (Almost) Everything*

⤳

The Examen is a prayerful, quick, 5-step review of your day. For me, it is a chance to remember that God is not far away but is vitally interested in everything I do, big and small. As time goes by I also find myself looking for God during the day instead of only remembering to do it at the end. That's a side benefit to the Examen.

I actually do the sort of mental replay that James Martin mentions above. It also gets me out of the rut I can fall into when I'm praying. Despite being a routine, the Examen stays fresh and interesting because it is an ever-changing encounter with God.

⤳

Dear Lord, thank you for the infinite variety of ways I can encounter you.

In My Day? ❧

1. Become aware of God's presence.

2. Review the day with gratitude.... Walk through your day in the presence of God and note its joys and delights.

3. Pay attention to your emotions. Reflect on the feelings you experienced during the day. What is God saying through these feelings?

4. Choose one feature of the day and pray from it. Ask the Holy Spirit to direct you to something during the day that *God* thinks is particularly important. It may be a vivid moment or something that seems rather insignificant. Pray about it..

5. Look toward tomorrow. Ask God to give you light for tomorrow's challenges.

End the Daily Examen with a conversation with Jesus. Ask forgiveness for your sins. Ask for his protection and help. Ask for his wisdom about questions or problems. Do all this in the spirit of gratitude. Your life is a gift, adorned with gifts from God.

Ignatian Spirituality website, Loyola Press

❧

I used to avoid doing the Examen because there are a lot of versions that focus on recalling what you've done wrong. I hated ending my day always feeling guilty.

This version surprised me because It had never occurred to me to ask God what he thought was important about my day (step 4). I can't tell you how curious and excited I am when I hit that step. Sometimes the memory is good and sometimes it is bad but it means so much because it is a real *conversation* with God. All in 15 minutes. That seems like a miracle, doesn't it?

ᴦ I ARISE TODAY

I arise today
Through God's strength to pilot me:
God's might to uphold me,
God's wisdom to guide me,
God's eye to look before me,
God's ear to hear me,
God's word to speak for me,
God's hand to guard me,
God's way to lie before me,
God's shield to protect me,
God's host to save me
From snares of devils,
From temptations of vices,
From everyone who shall wish me ill,
Afar and anear,
Alone and in multitude.

St. Patrick's Breastplate

ᴦ

St. Patrick's Breastplate is a long prayer. This is just a little piece of it. When I read it in the mornings it rolls off my tongue, preparing me for a day full of the Lord. It both shields me and prepares me.

ᴦ

Father, shield me today.

CHRIST WITH ME ~

Christ with me, Christ before me, Christ behind me,
Christ in me, Christ beneath me, Christ above me,
Christ on my right, Christ on my left,
Christ when I lie down, Christ when I sit down,
    Christ when I arise.

Christ in the heart and mind of every one who thinks of me,
Christ in the mouth of everyone who speaks of me or to me,
Christ in every eye that sees me or my works,
Christ in every ear that hears me or hears of me.

St. Patrick's Breastplate

~

I pray this often when I'm headed to a meeting. Or even just leaving the house. It's like putting on armor against the temptation to be awful to someone on the spur of the moment.

~

Christ, shine through all I do and may I meet you in everyone I encounter.

✣ Sacred Heart of Jesus

O Lord Jesus Christ, to your most Sacred Heart I confide this intention. Only look upon me, then do what your love inspires. Let your Sacred Heart decide. I count on you. I trust in you. I throw myself on your mercy. Lord Jesus, you will not fail me.

(Mention your request)

Sacred Heart of Jesus, I trust in you.

Sacred Heart of Jesus, I believe in your love for me.

Sacred Heart of Jesus, your kingdom come.

Sacred Heart of Jesus, I have asked you for many favors, but I earnestly implore this one. Take it, place it in your open heart. When the Eternal Father looks upon it, he will see it covered with your Precious Blood. It will no longer be my prayer, but yours, Jesus. Sacred Heart of Jesus, I place all my trust in you. Let me not be disappointed. Amen.

Traditional

↵

This is my very favorite novena*. There is something so moving in, "When the Eternal Father looks upon it, he will see it covered with your Precious Blood. It will no longer be my prayer, but yours, Jesus". It conveys a reality about Jesus' relationship to God the Father, and to me, which is beyond words.

*Novena comes from the Latin for "nine" and the novena tradition derives from the nine days when the apostles and Mary were praying in the upper room after Jesus ascended and before Pentecost.

I Place All My Trust in You ❧

The Lord himself will fight for you;
   you have only to keep still.

Exodus 14:14 (NAB)

Good is the Lord to one who waits for him,
   to the soul that seeks him.

Lamentations 3:25 (NAB)

❧

I have prayed many novenas in my day. It takes something desperate to prompt me to embark on such a prayer journey.

Sometimes God's answer is "yes." Sometimes is it is "no." Every time, remembering to say that prayer nine days in a row is more difficult than I thought it would be. Every time, it changes me for the better.

By the end of the nine days, the one sure thing I know is that we are not in control. We wait upon God's will and we must trust him to know what is best.

❧

Sacred Heart of Jesus, I place all my trust in you. I believe in your love for me.

⌁ Shallow Enough for a Lamb to Wade

There is no single way to pray. We pray as we can, not as we ought, yet it is good to remember that Christ most frequently speaks through His own words in Scripture. We pray to, in, and through Him. He is not somewhere else, but here now with me (you.)

Guigo II, *The Ladder of Monks*

Scripture is like a river again, broad and deep, shallow enough here for the lamb to go wading, but deep enough there for the elephant to swim.

St. Gregory the Great, Moralia, or a Commentary on Job

⌁

Christ voice rings out most loudly to me in scripture. A passage I've read a hundred times suddenly will glow with new depth. A well loved section suddenly has a sentence I don't recall having ever read before.

Each time, whether in a shallow or deep spot, the truth strikes my soul.

⌁

Oh how I love your law! It is my meditation all the day.

Psalm 119:97

Deep Enough for an Elephant to Swim ~

By reading the scriptures I am so renewed that all nature seems renewed around me and with me. The sky seems to be a pure, a cooler blue, the trees a deeper green. The whole world is charged with the glory of God and I feel fire and music under my feet.

Thomas Merton, *The Sign of Jonas*

It is a common temptation of Satan to make us give up the reading of the Word and prayer when our enjoyment is gone; as if it were of no use to read the Scriptures when we do not enjoy them, and as if it were no use to pray when we have no spirit of prayer.

George Müller, *A Narrative of Some of the Lord's Dealings with George Müller*

~

I have had revelations from reading scripture which seemed to tilt the earth on its axis, giving me a whole new way to see everything. Those moments are few and far between, however. Maybe that is why I need the reminder that reading scripture and praying is of use even when I don't "enjoy" them and it doesn't come easily.

When I dig in without worrying about what I will get out of it, that's when real change begins again.

~

In the way of your testimonies I delight as much as in all riches. I will meditate on your precepts and fix my eyes on your ways.

Psalm 119:14-15

⌁ Were Not Our Hearts Burning

Jesus said to them, "Oh, how foolish you are! How slow of heart to believe all that the prophets spoke! Was it not necessary that the Messiah should suffer these things and enter into his glory?" Then beginning with Moses and all the prophets, he interpreted to them what referred to him in all the scriptures. ...

Then they said to each other, "Were not our hearts burning [within us] while he spoke to us on the way and opened the scriptures to us?"

Luke 24: 25-27, 32

⌁

The road to Emmaus account (Luke 24:13-35) is my favorite resurrection story. Partly this is because God speaks to my heart very strongly through the written word. It often happens with scripture but can just as easily be through science fiction, mysteries, or even the newspaper.

So although it sounds odd, I pray through reading. I am grateful that God speaks to me in a way I can recognize.

⌁

Your word is a lamp to my feet and a light to my path.
Psalm 119:105 (RSV)

WHILE HE OPENED THE SCRIPTURES TO US? ∿

Reading, like a foundation, comes first: and by giving us the matter for meditation, it sends us on to meditation.

Meditation diligently investigates what is to be sought; it digs, so to speak, for treasure which it [then] finds and exposes: but since it is of itself powerless to obtain it, it sends us on to prayer.

Prayer, lifting itself with its whole strength to God, pleads for the desired treasure – the sweetness of contemplation.

[Contemplation's] advent rewards the labors of the other three; it inebriates the thirsty soul with the sweetness of heavenly dew.

Guigo II, The Ladder of Monks

For the word of God is living and active, sharper than any two-edged sword, piercing to the division of soul and of spirit, of joints and of marrow, and discerning the thoughts and intentions of the heart.

Hebrews 4:12 (RSV)

∿

Lectio Divina (Divine Reading) is an ancient way to pray with scripture. It's good for me to have Guigo's reminder above of the steps. Contemplation is the most difficult and the hardest to understand. It is what happens when we wait in stillness to see what God will say. It is what makes scripture come alive.

∿

My delight is in the law of the Lord, and I meditate on it day and night.

see Psalm 1:2

⌁ Could God Use Your Imagination

"Let me get this straight," I said. "You want me to make up a picture of the Gospel story in my head?"

David nodded.

"That's ridiculous," I said.

"What's ridiculous?"

"Isn't it all just in my head?" I asked. "Won't I just make the people in my fantasy do what I want them to do?" ...

"Let me ask you something," David said. "Do you believe that God gave you your imagination?"

"Sure," I said.

"Don't you think that God could use your imaginations to draw you closer to him in prayer?"

Father James Martin, *My Life With the Saints*

ↄ

I remember the first time I heard of this concept. I was instantly excited. This seemed not only easy but fun. It was both, which honestly isn't something you expect to say about prayer.

I don't know why I tend to forget this sort of meditation but it is yet another thing I have to be reminded about.

ↄ

Lord, receive my imagination and understanding. Enlighten me and draw me closer.

To Draw You Closer to Him in Prayer? ∿

First, take an episode from sacred Scripture. Take a scene from the gospels or any part of the Bible, and let your imagination go wild. Enter into it. Make the episode come alive by imagining you are there. Pretend you are part of it. ...

Second, pay attention to what happens. Who is in there? What are your sentiments? What are you saying to Jesus? What are you saying to Mary? What are you saying to the apostles? What are they saying to you?

Archbishop Timothy Dolan, *To Whom Shall We Go?*

ﻉ

Don't be contented with only conversation. Little details will help you enter into the scene more fully. What do you hear? Are there children nearby? Chickens scratching for bugs? What do you feel? The sun? Rough stones under your thin sandals? What do you smell? Is bread baking nearby? Are there flowers in the fields by the road?

Don't just listen or watch. Feel free to move about, help out in a scene, or talk to Jesus. It may not wind up being about the Gospel scene. That's the point of a real conversation, after all. You never know what twists and turns it will take.

ﻉ

Lord, receive my imagination and understanding. Enlighten me and draw me closer.

⌁ LOOK AT THIS TINY FACE

Imagine you are approaching that stable when Jesus was born. You hear the animals. Smell all the animal smells, good and bad. Feel the straw rustling as you step on it, see rough surfaces. And there is Mary. She smiles and you look at the baby who waves a fist in your direction. And then she puts the baby in your arms. Feel the weight of him. Look at this tiny face. He did this because he wants to get that close to you.

Father James Yamauchi, homily

… the hands that had made the sun and stars were too small to reach the huge heads of the cattle.

G. K. Chesterton, *The Everlasting Man*

↝

Here's one of the most basic examples in using imagination in prayer. I close my eyes and think about a real stable, a real baby, a real mother and father … and I'm there.

What happens next is up to God.

↝

Lord, receive my imagination and understanding. Enlighten me and draw me closer.

HE WANTS TO GET THAT CLOSE TO YOU ~

It was the first true cold snap of the season. I was wearing sweat pants and a jacket. In my mind's eye, Jesus strolled alongside. I was thinking over how my image of Jesus matched all those traditional pictures of the long dark hair and beard, the brown robe. I was shaking my head, "well, at least I realize I'm doing it."

I was completely caught off guard when "mind's eye Jesus" took the initiative.

"I suppose I have you to thank for this?" he said, laying a hand on the collar of a white T-shirt showing under the neck of his robe. "Keeping me warm?"

I snickered. I hadn't seen that in my "mind's eye" but it was colder than I thought a robe could handle.

"And these," he continued, sticking out a sandal shod foot from beneath the robe. Uncharacteristically, the sandal was on over a white tube sock, "are so my feet don't get cold?"

I couldn't help it. I howled with laughter. So glad that none of the other early walkers were around at that moment.

~

Yes, that really happened. On a walk. In my head. You gotta be careful who you let in there!

~

Thank you for the surprises and for having a sense of humor!

BATTLING EVIL

*Finding himself in the midst of the battlefield
man has to struggle to do what is right,
and it is at great cost to himself, and aided by God's grace,
that he succeeds in achieving his own inner integrity.*

Gaudium et spes
(Joy and Hope, Vatican II document)

~ My Soul Clings to You ~

I think of you upon my bed,
    and meditate on you in the watches of the night;
for you have been my help,
    and in the shadow of your wings I sing for joy.
My soul clings to you;
    your right hand upholds me.

Psalm 63:6-8 (NRSVCE)

⁓

In the midst of great distress and feeling as if I were under attack,
I flipped open my Bible and these verses sprang out at me. It
was as if God had taken my hand and calmed my spirit. I return
to them again and again for strength and as a reminder of God's
message to me.

⁓

In the shadow of your wings I sing for joy, Lord God.

◌ Satan Never Has and Never Will

Be sober, be watchful. Your adversary the devil prowls around like a roaring lion, seeking some one to devour.

1 Peter 5:8 (RSV)

One of the things that surprised me when I first read the New Testament seriously was that it talked so much about a Dark Power in the universe—a mighty evil spirit who was held to be the Power behind death and disease, and sin.

C. S. Lewis, Mere Christianity

◌

I assume that if you've gotten this far in this book you already know there really is such a person as Lucifer, the fallen angel we also call Satan, who rebelled against God and would like nothing more than to drag us all straight to Hell with him.

As convinced as I am of that very fact, I still sometimes fall prey to a completely secular way of thinking. I will forget all about evil, prowling like a roaring lion. It's a fine line between keeping evil in mind and becoming paranoid.

◌

Grant me the courage to do what I must when times are tough and the grace to know that I am in the center of your love.

Appear With Scars ~

Satan may appear in many disguises and at the end of the world will appear as a benefactor and philanthropist — but Satan never has and never will appear with scars.

Fulton Sheen, *Life of Christ*

It is the hands of God that caress us in our moments of sorrow, they comfort us. ... Jesus, God, took his wounds with him; he shows them to the Father. This is the price: the hands of God are wounded out of love. And this consoles us so much.

Pope Francis, *Encountering Truth*

↲

It never occurred to me to compare Jesus' scars to Satan who has never sacrificed anything for anyone and never will. Evil is real. There is no neutral ground. One way we can identify evil is by the lack of love, humility and sacrifice for others.

It's also how we tell which side our actions put us on. Do I love others as Jesus tells me to? How do I serve those around me? Do I have scars through my service, whether physical or otherwise? This is how I have to look at fighting evil. What am I willing to suffer for truth?

↲

Thank you for your sacrifice, for your wounds of love, dear Lord.

⤳ If the Victory Is Won

Only bad religion promises that God will put a bubble of protection around you. That's what got virgins thrown into volcanoes and it's what gets TV preachers rich. It's still a lie though, no matter how loudly or piously you say it.

What good religion teaches instead is that there is a Power at work in the world that is greater than the power of the world. It's a power that renews and restores. It heals ... It gives life ...

George Mason; Lakewood Advocate; September 29, 2014

⤳

Bad things will happen in life. No religion on earth can save us from that.

What our religion and our faith in Jesus Christ can save us from is trusting in the wrong thing. Jesus gave himself as a sacrifice to redeem us and also to show that there is something greater than the evils of the world.

⤳

Increase my faith, Lord Jesus. When bad times come, help me to remember that you have experienced it all before me. I trust you.

WHY DOES EVIL STILL PLAGUE US? ~

When things are crappy, and they often are, sometimes the best you can do is just turn up and do the will of God. That's what our Lord did and it was sometimes a pretty nasty experience. It's okay though, because the miserable part isn't the end of the story, is it?

Meanwhile, hold onto this thought: the Church is not a safe place. The Church is literally the front line between eternal good and absolute evil. It's going to look, feel, sound, and reek like a battlefield. If everything is always quiet on the front, you probably aren't on the front.

Jennifer Fitz, Sticking the Corners blog

~

Just showing up and doing God's will is how you get those scars of love, the way Jesus did. It's funny because the front lines are where all the fighting is, but if I'm on the right side then it is the safest place in the world — in the Father's will. I just have to hang on and do my bit.

~

Grant me the courage to do what I must when times are tough and the grace to know that I am in the center of your love.

◠ I Want You to Conquer

If we don't wish to be deceived, we must stay alert. If we want to overcome, we must fight. For this reason, the most wise Solomon says, "My son, if you come forward to serve the Lord ... prepare yourself for temptation" (Sirach 2:1).

Pope St. Leo I, Homily XXIX, 3

I let him tempt, through love, and not through hatred, because I want you to conquer, not be conquered, and to come to a perfect knowledge of yourself and of me.

God speaking to St. Catherine,
Dialogue of St. Catherine of Siena

◠

Why do I have to worry about temptation? Why can't God just help me out of my troubles? Sometimes it is because someone is exercising his free will, having lost his own struggle with temptation. Sometimes, and this seems harder to take, it is for our own good. It's like exercising. If we are never tested, whether in sports or puzzles or patience, how do we grow stronger — or know what we are capable of?

◠

Saint Michael the archangel, defend us in battle.
Be our safeguard against the wickedness and snares of the devil.
May God rebuke him, we humbly pray,
and do thou, O prince of the heavenly hosts, by the power of God,
Thrust into hell Satan
and all the evil spirits who prowl the world seeking the ruin of
*   souls.*
Amen.

Traditional

And Know Yourself and Me ~

When the devil can't deceive through stealth, he threatens explicitly and openly, holding out the fear of violent persecution to vanquish God's servants. He's always restless and always hostile, crafty in peace and fierce in persecution.

St. Cyprian of Carthage, On Jealousy and Envy, 1-3

When tempted, invoke your Angel. He is more eager to help you than you are to be helped! Ignore the devil and do not be afraid of him: He trembles and flees at the sight of your Guardian Angel.

St. John Bosco

⌁

In other words there is no time when we don't need our guardian angel's help. I go through long periods when I forget I even have a guardian angel. I am glad that I've got someone watching my back when I forget about it ... and about him!

⌁

Guardian angel, thank you for your eager defense against the attacks of my enemy!

ᴥ From the Enemy Defend Me

Soul of Christ, sanctify me.
Body of Christ, save me.
Blood of Christ, inebriate me.
Water from the side of Christ, wash me.
Passion of Christ, strengthen me.
O good Jesus, hear me.
Within thy wounds hide me
Suffer me not to be separated from thee.
From the malicious enemy defend me.
In the hour of my death call me,
and bid me come unto thee
that with thy saints I may praise thee
forever and ever. Amen.

Traditional

ᴥ

The first time I encountered this prayer I was focused on the connection between Christ and me (Soul of Christ, sanctify me). It took time and encounters with adversaries, both human and spiritual, to make me look more closely at "within thy wounds hide me." Those are the wounds he himself suffered from human and spiritual adversaries.

When I am afraid, when I am suffering, this prayer not only strengthens me but it pulls me closer to Christ who was not afraid to battle evil.

ᴥ

Suffer me not to be separated from thee, dear Jesus.

While I Breathe I Pray ∾

Christian, dost thou see them on the holy ground,
How the powers of darkness rage thy steps around?
Christian, up and smite them, counting gain but loss,
In the strength that cometh by the holy cross.

Christian, dost thou feel them, how they work within,
Striving, tempting, luring, goading into sin?
Christian, never tremble; never be downcast;
Gird thee for the battle, watch and pray and fast.

Christian, dost thou hear them, how they speak thee fair?
Always fast and vigil? Always watch and prayer?
Christian, answer boldly: While I breathe I pray!
Peace shall follow battle, night shall end in day.

Well I know thy trouble, O my servant true;
Thou art very weary, I was weary, too;
But that toil shall make thee some day all Mine own,
At the end of sorrow shall be near my throne.

St. Andrew of Crete, ancient hymn

∾

This is a song we sing occasionally at Mass. I've always liked the
swinging rhythm of the words but it took coming across it in a
prayer book to make the words really sink in. When I focused on
the last verse it hit home hard. Yes, Christ went through all this too.
This encouragement comes from a saint who also found strength
in Christ's example.

∾

Read the prayer aloud, with gusto.

FINDING JESUS
THROUGH THE HOLY SPIRIT

⁓

But the Helper, the Holy Spirit,
whom the Father will send in my name,
will teach you all things
and remind you
of everything that I have told you.
John 14:26 (ISV)

∿ The Last Power We Understand ∿

The Spirit is the first power we practically experience, but the last power we come to understand.

Oswald Chambers, *Biblical Psychology*

The missions of the Son and the Holy Spirit are inseparable and constitute a single economy of salvation. The same Spirit who acts in the incarnation of the Word in the womb of the Virgin Mary is the Spirit who guides Jesus throughout his mission and is promised to the disciples. The same Spirit who spoke through the prophets sustains and inspires the Church in her task of proclaiming the word of God and in the preaching of the Apostles; finally, it is this Spirit who inspires the authors of sacred Scripture.

Pope Benedict XVI, *Verbum Domini*

∿

Inseparable from Jesus' mission? Holy moly, look at how inseparable the Holy Spirit is from everything that helps us know who God is at all.

And yet often people forget all about the Holy Spirit. Let's admit it. He can seem pretty tough to relate to. But if he's on a mission of salvation, to save our souls, we shouldn't ignore him. Let's see about getting a little closer to him and Jesus both.

∿

Come, Holy Spirit. Fill my heart. Help me to know you better.

ᔥ God is Dynamic, Pulsating Activity

... in Christianity God is not a static thing — not even a person — but a dynamic, pulsating activity, a life, almost a kind of drama. Almost, if you will not think me irreverent, a kind of dance. The union between the Father and the Son is such a live concrete thing that this union itself is also a Person. I know this is almost inconceivable, but look at it thus. You know that among human beings, when they get together in a family, or a club, or a trade union, people talk about the "spirit" of that family, club, or trade union. They talk about its "spirit" because the individual members, when they are together, do really develop particular ways of talking and behaving which they would not have if they were apart (this corporate behavior may, of course, be either better or worse than their private behavior). It is as if a sort of communal personality came into existence. Of course, it is not a real person: it is only rather like a person. But that is just one of the differences between God and us. What grows out of the joint life of the Father and Son is a real Person, this Person is in fact the Third of the three Persons who are God.

C. S. Lewis, *Mere Christianity*

ᔤ

The Holy Spirit is the third person of the Holy Trinity and is God. He proceeds from the Father and the Son. This is hard to understand and probably one of the reasons he's often forgotten. That's why I like C. S. Lewis's example of the "spirit" of a family or group. I know exactly what he means. It helps me grasp the concept a little better.

ᔤ

Holy Spirit, guide my understanding.

Almost a Kind of Dance ~

The Holy Spirit rests in the soul of the righteous just like the dove in her nest. He hatches good desires in a pure soul, as the dove hatches her young.

St. John Vianney

Enrich your soul in the great goodness of God: The Father is your table, the Son is your food, and the Holy Spirit waits on you and then makes His dwelling in you.

St. Catherine of Siena

~

When something is as hard to grasp as the Holy Spirit, people use a lot of symbols and names trying to describe the indescribable. That can take a lot of different words: Helper, Comforter, Advocate, Counsellor, spirit, wind, dove, and flame are just a few.

I remember being delighted when I began finding the Holy Spirit's fingerprints all over my Bible. Scriptures brim with the Holy Spirit, from the Spirit moving over the face of the waters in Genesis, to the fire from heaven that Elijah's prayer called down, to the dove at Jesus' baptism, and the Helper he said God would send when he was gone.

Where has the Holy Spirit shown up that I haven't noticed? I need to pay more attention from now on.

~

Holy Spirit, open my eyes and heart to your presence.

✣ The Meaning

Come Holy Spirit.
Let the precious pearl of the Father
and the Word's delight come.
Spirit of truth,
    You are the reward of the saints,
            the comforter of souls,
            the light in the darkness,
            riches to the poor,
            treasure to lovers,
            food for the hungry,
            comfort to the wanderer;
    you are the one in whom all treasures are contained.

Come! As you descended on Mary,
that the Word might become flesh
work in us through grace.
Amen.

St. Mary Magadelen dei Pazzi

ↄ

A different phrase strikes me every time I pray this. It is all so true and I have needed these truths so many times.

The one that continually sparks my imagination, though, is "as you descended on Mary … work in us through grace." I think of gentle dew falling so lightly that you don't know it is there, until you look around and see it glistening. That gentle act of grace is how the Holy Spirit works in my soul. I can relax and let myself trust that this is true peace and comfort.

ↄ

Reflect upon the prayer above.

OF TRUE COMFORT ~

There is a saying: "Send out Thy spirit and all things will be created and Thou wilt renew the face of the earth." Do you realize that is true? ... What was real before still remains, yet everything has been renewed. Then you become aware that you have a heart and that it is given to you too to love, and things are filled with a gentle and holy meaning and you know: everything is good and it is worthwhile, divinely worthwhile, to be alive and to persevere.

When this happens to us — and the Lord promised that it would happen to us when He promised us the Comforter — we realize the meaning of true comfort.

Romano Guardini, The Living God

~

This and the prayer on the opposite page are two ways of saying the same thing. It is why I saw everything with new eyes after I entered the Church.

I feel that gentle, loving comfort and I know it is true. The Holy Spirit is in us and with us and brings us renewal, freshness, and joy.

~

Come Holy Spirit. Live within my heart.

⌁ BREAKING THAT HARDNESS OF HEART

To be sure, it is Christ who is seen, the visible image of the invisible God, but it is the Spirit who reveals him.

Catechism of the Catholic Church, 689

And I will give them one heart, and put a new spirit within them. And I will take the heart of stone out of their flesh and give them a heart of flesh, that they may walk in my statutes and keep my ordinances and do them. Then they will be my people, and I shall be their God.

Ezekiel 11:19-20 (RSV)

⌁

I signed up for a retreat in 2003 because I was looking for something to help me feel closer to Jesus. It did help some. But what really happened was a complete surprise.

Toward the end of our six-month spiritual formation after the retreat, one of my daughters asked a retreat friend to answer questions as part of her confirmation preparations. My friend suddenly looked up and said, "I wouldn't have answered these questions about the Holy Spirit this way at all before the retreat. But I just realized what a good friend He's become." I only then realized that what she said had happened to me too.

I came looking for Jesus and found the Holy Spirit. Who helps me to find Jesus. I guess the Spirit does reveal him just like the Catechism says.

⌁

Come Holy Spirit. Help me to know and love Jesus more.

And Making It Soft ~

You can follow a thousand catechism courses, a thousand spirituality courses, a thousand yoga or zen courses and all these things. But none of this will be able to give you the freedom as a child (of God). Only the Holy Spirit can prompt your heart to say "Father." Only the Holy Spirit is capable of banishing, of breaking that hardness of heart and making it ... soft? No, I don't like that word ... "docile." Docile towards the Lord. Docile when it comes to the freedom to love.

Pope Francis; homily Sept. 1, 2015

ﮯ

Pope Francis may hate the word soft but I don't. It describes precisely what happened when God got ahold of me. I had a heart like a stone and he softened it up.

I don't know exactly when it happened but it definitely accelerated after I went on that retreat. The Holy Spirit works softly and slowly, but you can't make room for God in your heart and expect it to stay the same.

Docile isn't a bad word. I don't mind it. And heaven only knows I work on my docility. But I can't be docile if my heart isn't softened up first. Whatever word you use, the bottom line is that the Holy Spirit leads us to love.

ﮯ

Come Holy Spirit. Thank you for being my helper, counsellor, friend.

Jesus
in the Holy Trinity

*The whole Christian life is a communion
with each of the divine persons,
without in any way separating them.
Everyone who glorifies the Father does so
through the Son in the Holy Spirit;
everyone who follows Christ does so
because the Father draws him
and the Spirit moves him.*

Catechism of the Catholic Church, *259*

ᴥ Trinity and My Little Head ᴥ

There's a legend that one day Augustine was walking along the beach at Hippo, his diocese in North Africa. He was trying to figure out the mystery of the Trinity. And as he moved along, he saw a boy running back and forth from the surf, carrying water in a bucket and pouring it into a small hole in the sand.

Augustine was curious. He asked the child what he was doing. The boy responded: "I'm pouring all that water" — meaning the ocean — "into this hole." Augustine said: "That's impossible. The ocean is huge, and your hole in the sand is tiny." The boy responded: "Then how can you expect to put the mystery of the Holy Trinity into that little head of yours?" And then the boy disappeared.

Archbishop Charles J. Chaput, "Called to Live in the Holy Spirit"

ᵔ

The Holy Trinity is a central mystery of the Christian faith and "mystery" is the operative word here. It really can make my head hurt if I try to puzzle it out. On the other hand, there is something about that holy mystery that also elevates my soul, makes me adore our unfathomable God, and love Jesus more than ever for taking on human flesh to help us find the way.

We'll just dabble our toes in that great ocean for a few pages to get a glimpse of the Trinity which is Jesus' nature.

ᵔ

O Most Holy Trinity, I adore Thee who are dwelling by Thy grace within my soul.

Traditional prayer to the Trinity, line 1

↜ If You Do Understand

The Trinity is One. ... We do not confess three Gods, but one God in three persons, the "consubstantial Trinity." The divine persons do not share the one divinity among themselves but each of them is God whole and entire.

The divine persons are really distinct from one another. "God is one but not solitary." ... they are really distinct from one another: "He is not the Father who is the Son, nor is the Son he who is the Father, nor is the Holy Spirit he who is the Father or the Son."

The divine persons are relative to one another. Because it does not divide the divine unity, the real distinction of the persons from one another resides solely in the relationships which relate them to one another ... the Father is related to the Son, the Son to the Father, and the Holy Spirit to both.

Catechism of the Catholic Church, 253-255

↝

God is infinitely complex and not limited to any dimensions whatsoever. We are three-dimensional creatures struggling to understand him. No wonder it's confusing. Sometimes I have a tiny glimpse of understanding. Struggling with this doctrine usually reminds me of what God told St. Catherine of Siena: "Do you know, daughter, who you are, and who I am? If you know these two things, you will be blessed."

I know the answer to that one. He's God. I'm not. That knowledge in itself is a blessing.

↝

O Most Holy Trinity, who art dwelling by Thy grace within my soul, make me love Thee more and more.

Traditional prayer to the Trinity, line 2

Then It Is Not God ～

We are talking about God. What wonder is it that you do not understand? If you do understand, then it is not God.

St. Augustine, Sermon 117

[God] is the Creator and merciful Father; he is the Only-Begotten Son, eternal Wisdom incarnate, who died and rose for us; he is the Holy Spirit who moves all things, cosmos and history, toward their final, full recapitulation. Three Persons who are one God because the Father is love, the Son is love, the Spirit is love.

God is wholly and only love, the purest, infinite and eternal love. He does not live in splendid solitude but rather is an inexhaustible source of life that is ceaselessly given and communicated.

Pope Benedict XVI, Solemnity of the Most Holy Trinity 2009

～

Even if it isn't easy, or might be completely impossible, it is still a good thing to occasionally grapple with tough ideas. It's how I stretch my mind and heart. It's how I grow closer to God.

Pope Benedict's commentary brings the Catechism definitions to life. I especially love the reminder that God does not live in solitude. What a glorious reflection on the Trinity and the continual flow of love therein. It reminds me that God is a person to be loved, not a series of definitions to learn.

～

O Most Holy Trinity, who art dwelling by Thy grace within my soul, sanctify me more and more.

Traditional prayer to the Trinity, line 3

❧ Wherever There is Love

"Who are you?" asked Shasta.

"Myself," said the Voice, very deep and low so that the earth shook: and again "Myself," loud and clear and gay: and then the third time "Myself," whispered so softly you could hardly hear it, and yet it seemed to come from all round you as if the leaves rustled with it.

C. S. Lewis, *The Horse and His Boy*

↶

You don't have to know anything about C. S. Lewis's Narnia books or the lion Aslan to hear echoes of the Holy Trinity in the passage above.

My favorite example of the Trinity is the legend of St. Patrick's explanation to the pagans. He used the shamrock, that most Irish of symbols. Each leaf represented one of the three persons, but yet it was still only one shamrock. It's the example that leaps to mind first when I'm asked about this very difficult doctrine.

I love finding different examples that give me insights into the Trinity. They don't always hold up on all levels, because they are examples of the ineffable, but they light one more little candle as I peer in the dark. They give me joy.

↶

Abide with me, O Lord; be Thou my true joy.
Traditional prayer to the Trinity, line 4

There is a Trinity ~

Wherever there is love, there is a trinity: a lover, a beloved, and a fountain of love.

St. Augustine, On the Trinity

The strongest proof that we are made in the image of the Trinity is this: love alone makes us happy because we live in a relationship, and we live to love and to be loved. Borrowing an analogy from biology, we could say that imprinted upon his "genome" the human being bears a profound mark of the Trinity, of God as Love.

Pope Benedict XVI, Solemnity of the Most Holy Trinity 2009

~

The ocean and that tiny hole didn't overwhelm St. Augustine completely because he went on to write about the Trinity in depth. His statement above is both the deepest and simplest I've ever read on the topic.

Whatever we do or don't understand, the one truth we can cling to is that we are made to love and be loved. This is what God created us for, this is what Jesus came to show us, and this is what the Holy Spirit whispers to our hearts each day.

If I can live in that love and show that love, then I am holding onto the reality of the Holy Trinity. And that is probably all I really need to know.

~

I believe in you, I hope in you, I love you, And I adore you,
O Blessed Trinity, one God; have mercy on me now and at the
hour of my death and save me. Amen.

Act of Faith

CONTINUING TO SEEK

ر

To fall in love with God is the greatest romance;
to seek him the greatest adventure;
to find him, the greatest human achievement.
Father Raphael Simon, O.C.S.O.

⌁ If the Vision Seems Slow

I will stand at my guard post,
    and station myself upon the rampart,
And keep watch to see what he will say to me,
    and what I will answer concerning my complaint.
And the Lord answered me:
    "Write the vision;
            make it plain upon tablets,
            so he may run who reads it.
For still the vision awaits its time;
    it hastens to the end—it will not lie.
If it seem slow, wait for it;
    it will surely come, it will not delay.

Habakkuk 2:1-3

⌁

Here is the rest of what Habakkuk says after he begins waiting upon the ramparts, the place where we began this prayer book.

I love the Lord's answer: Be patient. I haven't forgotten you. It just takes time. All will happen as it should.

The business of getting to know anyone takes a lot of time and many encounters. Knowing and loving our Lord is the same. I must be patient. And persistent.

⌁

Thank you, Lord, for your patience when I am impatient. Thank you for your faithfulness in answering every prayer, even when they are complaints.

WAIT FOR IT ～

Keeping a journal has taught me that there is not so much new in your life as you sometimes think. When you reread your journal you find out that your latest discovery is something you already found out five years ago. Still it is true that one penetrates deeper and deeper into the same ideas and experiences.

Thomas Merton, The Sign of Jonas

Creation has its own goodness and proper perfection, but it did not spring forth complete from the hands of the Creator. The universe was created "in a state of journeying" *(in statu viae)* toward an ultimate perfection yet to be attained, to which God has destined it.

Catechism of the Catholic Church, 302

～

Like Thomas Merton, I have discovered that once is not enough. Like the universe, I am "in a state of journeying" yet to be attained. I really love knowing that God is satisfied to let me … and the universe … find our own way to the destiny he has waiting. It shows his love, his delight in his creation, and, most important to me, his trust in how I will use my freedom.

I must contemplate things over and over to begin to grasp them deeply. It is a slow process but, looking back, I can see growth.

I am closer than I was to being able to answer Jesus' question, "Who do you say I am?" But I am still so far away.

So I must continue to seek. If it means beginning again at the beginning, then so be it. Back to the front of the book!

～

Thomas Merton, angels and saints, pray for me.

⌁ ADDITIONAL QUOTES ⌁

These are quotes which also inspire me to contemplation of
Jesus but which I couldn't fit into the book. I offer them for your
meditations in the hopes that they will spark a connection as they
do for me.

⌁

Nothing seems tiresome or painful when you are working for
a Master who pays well; who rewards even a cup of cold water
given for love of Him.

St. Dominic Savio

In all the world there is nothing so curious and so interesting
and so beautiful as truth.

Hercule Poirot in Murder in Three Acts by Agatha Christie

We are what we pretend to be, so we must be careful about what
we pretend to be.

Kurt Vonnegut, *Mother Night*, introduction

When you accept the fact of God, you simultaneously admit
your responsibility toward all creation. There is no such thing
as a private act.

John Aurelio

No man chooses evil because it is evil; he only mistakes it for
happiness, the good he seeks.

Mary Wollstonecraft, *A Vindication of the Rights of Men*

At the beginning of my spiritual life, at the age of about thirteen or fourteen, I asked myself what I should learn later; I then thought it impossible for me to understand perfection better; but I realized very quickly that the further one advances along this road the further from the goal one believes oneself to be.

Thérèse of Lisieux, *Story of a Soul*

An equation means nothing to me unless it expresses a thought of God.

Srinivasa Ramanujan, Indian mathematician, 1887-1920

This is what the past is for! Every experience God gives us, every person He puts in our lives is the perfect preparation for the future that only He can see.

Corrie Ten Boom, *The Hiding Place*

There are no "if's" in God's world. And no places that are safer than other places. The center of His will is our only safety — oh Corrie, let us pray that we may always know it!

Corrie Ten Boom, *The Hiding Place*

There's always a choice. That's God's way, always will be. Your will is still free. Do as you will. There's no set of leg irons on you. But ... this is what God wants.

Stephen King, *The Stand*

Oh, what a great book for us is the cross! It is a summarization of the apologetics of our faith, a practical knowledge for our moral life, and the most tender lesson of love that the Lord has shown.

St. Gaspar del Bufalo

Before we commit a sin, Satan assures us that it is of no consequence; after we commit a sin, he persuades us that it is unforgivable.

Fulton Sheen, The Priest is Not His Own

What do we live for, if it is not to make life less difficult for each other?

George Eliot, Middlemarch

Connection is why we're here. It's what gives purpose and meaning to our lives. ... In order for connection to happen, we have to allow ourselves to be seen. Really seen.

Brené Brown, "The Power of Vulnerability," TED talk

Regret doesn't remind us we did badly. It reminds us that we know we can do better.

Kathryn Schulz, "Don't Regret Regret," TED talk

But if the power of sin, death and evil has been broken, how can we make sense of the fact that it still continues to plague us? ... The victory won over sin through the death of Christ was like the liberation of an occupied country from Nazi rule. ... In one sense, victory has not come; in another, it has.

Alister E. McGrath, What Was God Doing on the Cross?

⤳ About the Author ⤝

Raised by atheists but always seeking, Julie Davis converted to Catholicism in 2000 and began blogging at Happy Catholic in 2004. She and her husband live in Dallas, Texas, where they have have worked together at their graphic design firm for 30 years. They have two grown daughters.

Julie's other books are available through Amazon:

- *Happy Catholic: Glimpses of God in Everyday Life*
- *Lord, Open My Heart: Daily Scriptural Reflections for Lent*

Connect with Julie online at:

- Happy Catholic - where she's not always happy but always happy to be Catholic. (happycatholic.blogspot.com)
- A Good Story is Hard to Find - a podcast where Scott Danielson and I talk "… about books, movies and traces of 'the One Reality' we find there." (agoodstoryishardtofind.blogspot. com)